For Martha, Sarah, and Ellen

"Do not neglect to show hospitality to strangers, for by doing that some have entertained angels without knowing it."

HEBREWS 13:2

Contents

~

Preface to the 2008 Edition   vii

Introduction   ix

1. **Describing the Christian Life**   1

   Changing Understandings   4

   A Life Given in Worship   9

   Roman Catholic and Protestant Perspectives   14

2. **An Anglican Perspective**   25

   Faith as a Way of Life   29

   The Theological Tradition   35

   Theology and Ethics   43

3. **Incarnate Love**   53

   The Transformation of Sexuality   54

   Idolatry and Moralism   63

   The Covenant of Hospitality   69

4. **Love and Justice**   **77**

  The Transformation of Poverty   *80*

  The Nature of Justice   *89*

  Law and Gospel   *94*

5. **The Practices of Faith**   **103**

  Disciplines of Mind and Body   *105*

  Worship and the Disciplines of Faith   *114*

  Hospitality and Forgiveness   *122*

6. **The Call of God**   **127**

  The Nature of Calling   *128*

  The Faith of Piety   *135*

  Ethics and the Christian Life   *138*

Appendix   **143**

  Theology as Grounded in Piety   *144*

  Narrative Theology and Practice   *150*

  Understandings of God   *154*

Index   **159**

Preface to the 2008 Edition

❧

*T*HE CHRISTIAN MORAL LIFE seeks to offer an account of the
Christian life. It is in this sense that the word "piety" is used. Practices of piety refer not narrowly to spiritual practices but—as the word
"piety" originally meant—to our duties that bind us to God, to our
neighbors, and to our true selves. Christian ethics as reflection on the
Christian life are not then narrow and separate disciplines concerned
with right action (whether in terms of ends, virtues, or principles),
but are grounded in our encounter with God and the practices that
witness, nurture, and shape our continuing relationship with God. In
this sense, *The Christian Moral Life* is formed in conversation with theology and with what has been traditionally called ascetical theology
and what is now referred to more frequently as Christian spirituality
or Christian practices—hence the subtitle, *Practices of Piety.*

In the Roman Catholic tradition moral theologies came to be
more narrowly focused on offering direction to confessors in order
that they might help penitents in the confession of sins and offer
appropriate judgment and counsel. However, moral theologies from
Thomas Aquinas to Barnard Haring have sought more comprehen-
sively to ground moral principles and specific moral judgments in
understandings of the end of human life in God, the nature of the
human person, and human virtues grounded in relationship to God,
all placed in the context of the sacramental, worshipping community of faith.

In this sense *The Christian Moral Life* seeks to offer a moral theology, grounded, however, in a renewed sense of the worshipping

community. The understanding of the worshipping community in relationship to the world can no longer be taken-for-granted, as it was in the writing of traditional moral theologies when Christianity was established, what we call Christendom. Instead, the community of worship offers an alternative world, a sign of who we are meant to be, revealed in Scripture and known in the life of the community of faith as marked by its worship. So Edward Schillebeeckx's sacramental principle: as Christ is the sacrament of God to the world, the church is the sacrament of Christ.[1]

The traditional elements of moral theology are then addressed in *The Christian Moral Life* within this larger context. There is an account of cardinal and theological virtues. These are grounded in an account of the encounter with God as a matter of hospitality to the stranger. Moral principles are developed as expressing the ends of action. And traditional questions are addressed, for example, the relationship between the love of God and neighbor, the first and the second table of the Ten Commandments, law and gospel, and love and justice. And this leads to the practices of piety, the nature of vocation, and the mission of God.

As I look back to my initial explorations of these matters in *Sacramental Ethics: Paschal Identity and the Christian Life* (Fortress, 1987) and ahead to *Preaching What We Practice: Proclamation and Moral Discernment* (Morehouse, 2007), with David Schlafer, I see how much my own work has explored what has been central to the great Anglican moral theologian Kenneth Kirk, from *Some Principles of Moral Theology* (Longmans, Green, 1920) and *Conscience and Its Problems: An Introduction to Casuistry* (Longmans, Green, 1927) to *The Vision of God* (Longmans, Green, 1928). The difference has been in casting the character of a Christian ethic in a post-Christendom world grounded in liturgical and sacramental theology. Here again, in Anglicanism this grounding in the worshipping community is prefaced by the first book to introduce the liturgical renewal movement in the English world, A.G. Hebert's *Liturgy and Society* (Faber and Faber, 1935). *The Christian Moral Life* has this twentieth-century lineage. I hope that it may prompt its continued engagement and development.

---

[1] Edward Schillebeeckx, *Christ: The Sacrament of the Encounter with God,* tr. *Paul Barrett* (New York: Sheed and Ward, 1963).

Introduction

◈

I HAVE BEEN fortunate to share in the worship of a variety of Christian churches. The power of those experiences has confirmed that the presence of God given in worship is inseparable from the call into the covenant of hospitality that is our daily life. I recall worship with a variety of Christian communities: with an Anabaptist community of Brethren during Holy Week where I shared with them foot washing and an agape meal; with an African-American congregation in the preaching and singing which drew out the congregation together in praise and in petitions for the world; with a Roman Catholic community of Benedictine monks in singing the daily offices as they have since the fourth century; with Quakers in the quiet stillness in their meeting; with Presbyterians in Sunday worship with prayers offered in response to scripture and the sermon; with Eastern Orthodox in their divine liturgy with incense rising, intoned prayers, and blessings; with an ecumenical group in reading scripture and offering prayer together; and with my seminary community in daily worship.

When I think about what is central to all such worship, I remember a Sunday Eucharist in China following the opening of China after the cultural revolution. The service was ecumenical in a reopened church without windows. I could not understand the Chinese, but the shape of the Eucharist drew me into the participation we call worship. That evening at dinner I sat next to an 83-year-old minister, a Chinese man who was formerly a Seventh Day Adventist. We talked about the changes sweeping China and we talked about the church. I asked him how his own faith and understanding of the church had changed since the Chinese Revolution in 1949. He said simply, "We were wrong before. We thought more of our churches than of faith. Our effort was to preserve the church. Now we share one church because we know that we are the church only if we serve all people."

Nothing could express more clearly to me the nature of Christian faith. My Anglican roots have enabled me to see this vision of faith. But it is only in my own encounter and the consequent welcome and embrace of strangers — of their embrace of me and of my embrace of them — that I have known this life. From this comes an ecumenical spirit. The church is not the end of faith. Instead, the end of the church is God's calling, to enable the voice of God that it may be heard calling all people into a covenant of hospitality.

As I was concluding this book I reread H. Richard Niebuhr's *The Purpose of the Church and Its Ministry*[1] and was aware of how much my own work, beginning with my doctoral dissertation on H. Richard Niebuhr, has been a working out of questions he pursued. Through now 20 years of seminary teaching my concern has been on the experience of God and on the mediation and deepening of faith as a matter of response to that experience. The questions that have haunted me are, "How is God present in our lives?" and "How does the church enable our relationship to God, especially in the radically pluralistic, secular world we call postmodern?" These are questions central to Niebuhr's work, especially as he saw institutional churches as the bearers of Christian faith but also assimilated into the prevailing culture.

The church, of course, is not one thing but highly varied and, as monastics and Protestant reformers both saw, always in need of being reformed. Niebuhr, for example, asked, at one point, does the church

1. H. Richard Niebuhr, *The Purpose of the Church and Its Ministry* (New York: Harper & Row, 1954).

need to go "Back to Benedict?"[2] In one sense, I am convinced that it does. Only through spiritual disciplines of reading scripture, prayer, and acts of hospitality will persons form a way of life in which the Christian story makes sense and the experience of God is deepened. Such a renewal of Christian life is the larger purpose of this book. The more particular purpose is the development of a Christian ethic that would have at its center the deepening of the encounter with God. In this way, this book is the development of Christian ethics as "sacramental ethics."[3]

In this book I have worked in two steps. In the first two chapters I have sought to offer an introduction to Christian ethics in general and Anglican understandings in particular. Central understandings of Christian faith and life have been identified. In the subsequent chapters I have sought to move from historical understandings to a contemporary account of the Christian moral life, at least as I am able to as a "cradle born" Episcopalian who has had some opportunity to know others in and outside of Anglican churches.

Both parts of this introduction focus on the fact that this way of life we call Christian is a life lived in our relationship to the world about us: to those near at hand, neighbors, with whom we share daily life, and to those who are "other" than ourselves, strangers. As suggested in understanding Christian faith as a practical piety, Christian faith is a life lived in which a person is opened to the world-at-hand, drawn out and connected to a world beyond oneself. This is a life of turning, of conversion, from life given and defined by particular and often individualistic desires for fulfillment to a new life given as a member of a people who live life in the embrace of others. Finally, as both parts of this book emphasize, the Christian life is grounded in the experience and worship of God. Worship is central to the life of Christian faith in the sense that worship is the celebration and deepening of the experience of God in our lives.

2. H. Richard Niebuhr, "Back to Benedict?" *The Christian Century* 42 (July 2, 1925): 860-61.

3. Timothy F. Sedgwick, *Sacramental Ethics: Paschal Identity and the Christian Life* (Philadelphia: Fortress Press, 1986).

INTRODUCTION

This account of the Christian life has developed through a variety of conversations. These conversations have been centered in the church, specifically in seminary and parish. I am thankful for 19 years at Seabury-Western Theological Seminary and St. Luke's Parish in Evanston, Illinois. Conversations from classroom (especially a class called "The Christian Life") to parish hall have been the birthplace of this book. I am also thankful for the opportunity to continue these conversations and complete this writing at my new home at Virginia Theological Seminary in Alexandria, Virginia.

This book, though, would not have been possible apart from the extended church and especially invitations to offer earlier attempts to give an account of the moral life. I am grateful to the Rev. Mike Adams and the Church of the Ascension for the opportunity to offer the inaugural Lyle Parratt Lectures in Lafayette, Louisiana; to Union Theological Seminary in Richmond, Virginia, and especially then Dean Charles Swezey, for the invitation to give five lectures on "The Practice of the Christian Life" for the Faith Continuing Education Week; to the Rev. John Andrews and the parish of St. Gabriel-the-Archangel, Englewood, Colorado, for a further opportunity to lecture on the Christian life; and to the Rev. Ray Coulter, the Rev. Anne Bartlett, and the Parish of St. John the Baptist, Portland, Oregon, for inviting me to give the endowed Greenfield Lectures.

A number of more focused occasions have also been important in the development of this introduction to the Christian life. These include teaching in the diocesan schools of Idaho and North Dakota; offering the Rossiter Lectures at Bexley Hall, the Episcopal seminary in Rochester, New York; giving lectures and leading discussion for a clergy conference for the Diocese of Central New York; giving two keynote addresses for the National Gathering of Lay Professionals in New Orleans; and addressing preaching the Christian life for the Annual Theology Conference sponsored by the ecumenical Metro-Toledo Churches United in Toledo, Ohio. I am thankful for these opportunities

Finally, there is no such thing as the solitary scholar. Work is always born by larger communities and colleagues, in this case academic and ecclesial. I am indebted and thankful to more people than I can name. Three individuals, however, stand out. The Rev. David Fisher has been a friend and scholarly conversation partner for more than 25 years. Our bi-monthly reading together in philosophy and theology has fueled my thoughts, especially in seeing that the question of identity is the question of difference. The Rev. Philip Turner has been my other extended conversation partner for 15 years. He has made me see ever more clearly that faith begins in practices which themselves are the point of entry into faith itself. Third, the Rev. Jim Griffiss read this book in its earliest draft and helped me see what needed development.

As all things are ultimately personal, I dedicate this account to the women in my life: Martha and our two daughters, Sarah and Ellen. This is the story of our life together.

CHAPTER 1

Describing the Christian Life

~

WHAT NEEDS to be done? What do I want to do? Who should I call? Who do I want to call? Our daily lives are given in the responses we make to such questions. We are most often aware of our responses in times of change. Change raises the question, "What is most important to us?" "What do we truly love and desire?"

My students often accuse me of asking "cosmic questions." The cosmic questions, however, are simply asking what is the pattern in the answers we give to the ordinary questions of our daily lives. How often I have heard such questions as these from my two daughters during their teenage years: What should I do today? What should I wear? Do I want to be by myself or go out with friends? Should I buy some new pants? Should I stay up and study some more or go to sleep now and study in the morning? What courses should I take? What am I going to do this summer? Our responses to such questions are much like sentences in the unfolding of a larger story. One sentence leads to the next. As we look back we discern a drama marked by different scenes, characters, and conflicts.[1]

1. The narrative understanding of ethics as a matter of setting, character, and plot has its origins in Aristotle's *Poetics*. See Paul Ricoeur, *Oneself as Another*, trans. Kathleen Blamey (Chicago: University of Chicago Press, 1992),

Deep guidance for the moral life cannot be gained by narrowly focusing on the crises of our daily lives. In asking what I should do this day, I can be helped by writing down a list of possibilities and then identifying what I like and dislike about each item. In focusing only on the decisions, however, I cannot understand what values and loves are most important to my life. Deep guidance can come only from an understanding of the stories that express the drama I see myself living. These range from my family stories to the stories given in the different cultures in which I live. In turn, I seek some story that both makes sense of my life's stories and expresses a larger meaning and purpose to which I can give myself. What makes understanding Christian faith and the moral life difficult are the different stories of Christian faith and life that have been offered.

Often I find our situation like living in a city where I encounter fragments of stories but do not know how these fit together. For example, in joining in Christian worship I sing songs that celebrate the death and resurrection of Jesus. These evoke another world, holy and full of mystery, given in silence and prayer. But making sense of prayer and this ancient language of sacrifice and blessing is something that involves deciphering. I hear in a sermon that I am baptized into a new life, and I feel something new in this community of worship. But I cannot make sense of what that means when I hear the radical demands in the gospel to sell everything and to come follow in Jesus' way. I sense something of the Christian story as a way of life, but I don't know how it fits with the other worlds of meaning and value in

---

p. 143. This has been the center of many contemporary understandings of the relationship of Christian faith and ethics. See, for example, Stanley Hauerwas and L. Gregory Jones, eds., *Why Narrative? Readings in Narrative Theology* (Grand Rapids: Eerdmans, 1989). Central to this development has been the work of Alasdair MacIntyre, especially *After Virtue: A Study in Moral Theory* (Notre Dame: University of Notre Dame Press, 1984) in which he argues that all ethics depend on a way of life grounded in a set of practices and understood in terms of a life story. Among the best accounts of the foundations that inform this work is William Schweiker, *Mimetic Reflections: A Study in Hermeneutics, Theology and Ethics* (New York: Fordham University Press, 1990). For a discussion of these foundations, see the Appendix.

which I live — providing for children, making a living, caring for myself, giving to the community, being with others, and being with myself. Understanding the Christian moral life is then first of all a matter of understanding the story of Christian faith as making sense of our life in the world.[2] The challenge of developing such an account is what I will call the problem of piety.

The word "piety" is often understood as devoutness, as religiousness, often with a pejorative sense of being narrow and judgmental. This is suggested by the phrase, "she is certainly a pious person." The word piety, however, has a far broader meaning. According to the *Oxford English Dictionary,* piety originally referred to persons who habitually acted with "reverence and obedience to God" and "faithfulness in the duties owed to parents and relatives [and] superiors."[3] The Anglican Jeremy Taylor described piety as a way of life more fully in his 1650 book on *The Rule and Exercise of Holy Living.* He structures the book itself in terms of sobriety, justice, and religion. Sobriety means "our deportment in our personal and private capacities, the fair treating of our bodies and spirits." Justice is a matter of "our duty to all relations to our neighbours." Religion refers to "the offices and direct religion and intercourse with God."[4] Altogether, sobriety, justice, and religion formed a way of life Taylor described as Christian piety. Such piety, he said, was a matter of a life formed in order to "stand before God, acting and speaking, and thinking in His presence."[5]

This understanding of piety as a way of life is what I mean by piety. I will often refer to such piety as practical piety in order to emphasize the practices that are central to piety. The question of an adequate account of the Christian life is then, "What is the character of Christian practical piety given the different pieties that we may encounter?"

---

2. This is the argument central to H. Richard Niebuhr's *Christ and Culture* (New York: Harper & Row, 1957).

3. *Oxford English Dictionary,* 2nd ed. (Oxford: Oxford University Press, 1991), vol. 11, p. 804.

4. Jeremy Taylor, *Holy Living and Holy Dying,* 2 vols., ed. P. G. Stanwood (Oxford: Clarendon, 1989), vol. 1, p. 29.

5. Taylor, *Holy Living and Holy Dying,* vol. 1, p. 3.

This challenge may be posed in terms of what I will call modern, postmodern, and traditional pieties.[6]

Changing Understandings

I grew up for the most part in the sprawling suburbs of Chicago following World War II. My world was formed by the promises of education, science, and technology. Polio could be prevented. I went for the series of vaccinations and never again heard speak the fear that I might catch polio by swimming in the public pool. In 1957 the Soviets sent Sputnik into orbit, and the United States entered the space race. Altogether, I was part of a generation educated to conquer new frontiers.

I assumed that life was about successfully meeting challenges and solving problems. The meaning and end of life for me were given in seeking to form a world in which the basic needs of all people would be met, where everyone had an equal opportunity to share in the challenges and the chance to form a better life. This was what writers in Christian ethics spoke of as fellowship, or, to use their patriarchal language, "the fatherhood of God and the brotherhood of man." My hope was a form of idealism. I conceived an ideal state of affairs and envisioned life as moving towards that ideal. Christian faith gave expression to the ideals of love and justice. It held the promise that people could change, that there was a grace in acceptance and forgiveness. The church for me was that community of grace; it invited me to participate in a larger purpose that gave dignity and value to life.

6. The following sketches of pieties are intended to reflect different types of responses. These types (traditional, modern, and postmodern) point to the transformation in worldviews and understandings from what might be called preenlightenment to modern to postmodern. For an account of the changes informing these sketches and, more broadly, the argument of this book in general, see Charles Taylor, *Sources of the Self: The Making of the Modern Identity* (Cambridge, Mass.: Harvard University Press, 1989); Steven Toulmin, *Cosmopolis: The Hidden Agenda of Modernity* (New York: Free Press, 1990); and Alasdair MacIntyre, *After Virtue.*

My idealism was broken by the failure of the United States in the 1960s and '70s to stop the war in Vietnam and to address the sources of poverty and racial oppression in American society. Martin Luther King's "Poverty March" on Washington, the assassinations of Robert Kennedy and Martin Luther King, the demonstration and riots at the 1968 Democratic convention in Chicago, the killing of student pro-testers at Kent State University following the expansion of the Viet-nam War into Cambodia: these made impossible the conviction that society would realize an ideal.

My own experience allowed me to hear other voices, from the survivors of the Jewish Holocaust to political refugees to those suffer-ing a slow death from terminal illness. The voice is constantly that of Kurt in Joseph Conrad's *Heart of Darkness* saying, "The horror, the horror." If there was any purpose that gave meaning to life, I came to believe that it had to be given in the very midst of human suffering and failure. This was for me most powerfully articulated by particular peoples: for example, African-Americans speaking of the "black expe-rience," of spirituals and blues that celebrated life in the midst of vio-lence and oppression.[7] Above all, these voices have meant for me that if there was any meaning that could redeem life, it would have to be simply there, given, the ground and basis for what I did, a matter of grace. Instead of images of a new Jerusalem, of the coming of the king-dom of God, my prayers have become more focused by Job and by Je-sus' suffering and death.

The change in my sense of life's meaning is more than my com-ing of age. Instead, my personal experiences reflect broader changes in the understandings of society and culture. The sense of value and meaning given in achieving a new and better society is what has been central to what is called a modern vision of things. Modern in this sense refers to what is called the legacy of the Enlightenment. Begin-ning in the eighteenth century, the developments of science and tech-nology gave confidence that through reason, human ingenuity, and sheer effort, nature could be tamed and the world could be perfected

---

7. Riggins Earl, *Dark Symbols, Obscure Signs: God, Self, and Community in the Slave Mind* (Maryknoll, N.Y.: Orbis, 1993).

so that all people could live together peaceably. In contrast, my sense of the broken and fragmentary character of life has been called a postmodern vision. Postmodern means after the modern, after the collapse of confidence in reason and progress. Both of these, modern and postmodern, stand in contrast to what may be called a traditional vision.

The traditional understanding of Christian faith and life was reflected in my grandparents. I think especially of my great-grandmother, who was born in 1882 in the newly settled land of southeastern Minnesota. Of all her grandchildren I was among the more inquisitive, always asking her to tell me what it was like before electricity and automobiles. She spoke matter-of-factly of changes and challenges. Homesteading, the final uprising of the Sioux, the move to the city, industrialization, economic depression, the World Wars, and before she died not only jet airplanes but landing on the moon — these were the background to her history. But what appears most basic from her earliest experience was the sense of need for order, discipline, and hard work. Each person was to do his or her duty at home and at work, in the community, and for society. Authority was taken for granted. Christian faith for her made sense of this ordered life in terms of the personal virtues of trust, honesty, industry, and integrity. These virtues were sustained by a sense of the divine as ordering and judging but also as merciful and forgiving. To say God was loving was to say that there was forgiveness for the failure to live up to the divine order.

This traditional piety did not create a narrow sense of the miserable sinner, but was rather a sober assessment of our lives. Sunday worship began with the confession of sin or, when Holy Eucharist was celebrated, with the reading of the Ten Commandments or at least a summary of the law and then the confession of sin. The centrality of the law in worship expressed a clear sense of order and, in turn, a sense of sin, of personal failing to live up to the demands of the law. In a world lacking basic security, people depended on mutual cooperation. Failure, for example, to keep one's word, to offer help as promised, could threaten the livelihood and even physical life of another person or of the community as a whole. The consequences of sin on the common life were visibly imagined, if not directly seen, and for this reason moral failure evoked sorrow and repentance — not narrowly a turning from evil deeds but more broadly a turning from a narrow self-concern. Repentance called forth God's mercy to uphold all people in a holy and righteous life, to grow continually in love and service. In and through Jesus Christ, God's mercy and blessing were assured. This traditional life of faith was not marked narrowly by duty. Instead, for the ordering of life and the means of grace that made it possible, there was a deep sense of gratitude that continued to turn individual lives outward beyond themselves. Duty and obligation were but the other side of love and care, which connected the individual to the larger human community.

These three pieties — traditional, modern, and postmodern — focus on different aspects of Christian faith and life and need not be seen as opposed to each other, as if one were right and another were wrong. The older, traditional piety of my grandmother focuses on a world defined by personal duties, so much so that from our own cultural vantage point they tend to be perceived as moralistic or rigid, focused excessively on individual relations and virtues. Christian faith arises in the experience of judgment regarding our failures. Such judgment, however, is not at its heart moralistic and individualistic. Rather, the judgment is a judgment of failure to participate in a larger order of things necessary for individuals to be a people. God's forgiveness is then an act that restores participation in that order. This is a justification by grace that, in turn, frees a person from self-absorbed individualism.

The modern piety of my young adulthood focused on the future. This emphasis arose in part because traditional piety seemed to have lost sight of the future and instead focused on duty, judgment, and mercy. To look at the future, though, was to see that reconciliation was a new creation, a community of love and justice. The larger sense of reconciliation — as corporate and incarnate, as becoming a people in this world — was restored. The human problem, however, was sometimes too narrowly thought of as human failure to live in God's kingdom, without attention to the actual dynamics that form human life together. The presence of God as a matter of judgment and a gift of grace was too easily lost from view.

Postmodern piety has turned attention back to the present. Born of the experience of God as the experience of sheer grace in the midst of suffering, the sense of the giftedness of life was restored. In turn, the human response to God was brought back into view as a matter of vulnerability and openness, of dependence and trust, of thanksgiving and compassion. The dynamics of turning to God, of conversion, were illumined. This focus on God's epiphany or manifestation in the midst of the breaking apart of life, however, can lose itself in the present. Apart from the roles, relations, and practices that lead to and from the encounter with God, the postmodern focus on experience can become individualistic and pluralistic, fragmentary and relativistic.

While these three pieties may share a common set of convictions, each of these pieties is distinct in its emphasis, because one is reacting to another. Traditional pieties, with their emphasis on duties and obligations, can lose touch with the larger ends of forming communities of love and justice. Modern pieties thus focus on ends and ideals but in doing so tend to de-emphasize duties and obligations. In turn, the idealism of such modern pieties may evoke a traditional reaction or else a postmodern turn back to the experience of grace in the life lived.

This description of three pieties is by no means an adequate account of the pieties that have formed different generations. It is not my intention to depict pieties simply as traditional, modern, and postmodern. My more limited purpose is to suggest the differences and tensions between different generations and different communities. If Christian ethics is to offer a broader understanding of Christian faith and life, the challenge of Christian ethics is to offer an account of Christian faith as a way of life, in spite of the differences among Christians. As a matter of faith, this means a Christian ethic must answer the question, "What is good, right, and holy?" As a matter of a way of life, a Christian ethic must answer a second and third question: "How do we come to know and how do we participate in this life?"[8] Differ-

---

8. This is a variation of the three questions by which James M. Gustafson has defined the discipline of theological ethics: What is the nature of the good? What is the nature of moral agency? And, what are the criteria for moral judgment? See James M. Gustafson, "Christian Ethics," *The Westminster Dictionary*

ent pieties initially appear to give different answers to these questions. A Christian ethic must find some common answer.

A Life Given in Worship

At the most obvious level, what the different Christian pieties share in common is that each is founded or grounded in Jesus. As the word "Christ" or "Messiah" originally meant, for Christians Jesus is the one who brings in the kingdom of God, the one who brings reconciliation and redemption. As such, Jesus is the divine messenger and agent who brings his followers, his disciples, into a new life. However, understandings of Jesus are as different as the pieties themselves. To those in darkness Christ is the light. To the guilty Christ brings forgiveness. To those in bondage Christ gives freedom. To those divided Christ is the reconciler. To those oppressed Christ liberates. To the broken Christ brings peace. Jesus enlightens, forgives, gives freedom, brings justice. Regardless of the image, Jesus is the Christ because he effects new life. At the same time, however, as the different images suggest, this new life has been described in different ways. The four gospels themselves reflect such differences. Again, the challenge in developing an account of the Christian moral life is to describe the shape and central features of a life that Christians share in common.

The Ten Commandments offer an initial point of reference for seeing what is central to the Christian moral life.[9] The Ten Commandments may serve as such a reference because they have been a

---

of Christian Ethics, James F. Childress and John Macquarrie, eds. (Philadelphia: Westminster, 1986), pp. 87-90. Also see James M. Gustafson, *Protestant and Roman Catholic Ethics* (Chicago: University of Chicago Press, 1978), esp. pp. 139-44.

9. For a historical and scriptural account of the development and meaning of the Ten Commandments see Walter J. Harrelson, *The Ten Commandments and Human Rights* (Philadelphia: Fortress, 1980). For a contemporary discussion in light of contemporary Christian ethics see Paul Lehmann, *The Decalogue and a Human Future* (Grand Rapids: Eerdmans, 1995).

central text for all Christians. They have provided the basic frame-work for Roman Catholic ethics — what Roman Catholics them-selves call moral theology. In Protestant churches they have been equally important. In his catechisms, for example, Luther exhorted Christians to read the Ten Commandments daily. In Anglican churches the Lord's Prayer, the Ten Commandments, and the Creed were displayed at the front of the church. For Anglicans, the Eucharist itself began with a reading of the entire Ten Command-ments or the summary of the law.

The Ten Commandments indicate the first major feature of the Christian moral life. Moral commands are grounded religiously. As the summary of the law says, "You shall love the Lord your God with all your heart, and with all your soul, and with all your mind. This is the greatest and first commandment. And a second is like it: You shall love your neighbor as yourself. On these two commandments hang all the law and the prophets." (Matt. 22:37-40; Mark 12:30-31; Luke 10:27)[10]

The Hebrew people understood and shared this understanding of the nature and purpose of law. Central to Judaism is Torah, a He-brew word used to designate the first five books of Hebrew Scripture, what for Christians is the Old Testament. Central to Judaism is giving thanks and delight in the Torah, that is, in the law. But the word *law* is misleading, at least to the extent that it narrowly focuses on acts as some means to an end. Instead, Torah more broadly means a way of

10. Here the purpose of law is understood in terms of love — love of God and love of neighbor as these two are integrally related. But, as indicated below in this chapter, the nature of love of God and neighbor is not clear. Love of God is not even mentioned in the Old Testament; in the New Testament, outside of the summary of the law, it is mentioned only one other time (Luke 11:42). As one line of thought this book is the development of such an understanding of divine and human love. For a summary of the reasons for the lack of such an account, and in turn a constructive account to which I am in basic agreement and with which this account coheres, see Edward C. Vacek, *Love, Divine and Human: The Heart of Christian Ethics* (Washington, D.C.: Georgetown University Press, 1994), pp. 131-33.

life detailed in law. This way of life itself arises from the law as people seek to deepen their relationship with God.[11]

At the heart of the Torah is the story of the Exodus and the giving of the commandments to Moses as he leads the Israelites out of slavery in Egypt into the land of Canaan in order to form a new people. Exodus is preceded by Genesis, the telling of creation and the beginnings of the Hebrew people as wandering nomads, heirs of Abraham, Isaac, and Jacob. In the other three books of the Torah (Leviticus, Numbers, and Deuteronomy), the Exodus story is extended. At the heart of this story are the commandments and codes governing worship, daily rituals, and moral and civic matters. These laws, however, are inseparable from the larger story of the Hebrews' relationship with God. The Ten Commandments are preceded by God simply declaring, "I am the Lord your God." Relationship is given. And this relationship is the basis for life: "I brought you out of the land of Egypt, out of the house of slavery" (Deut. 5:6). The commands express how to acknowledge and honor this relationship.

The first of the Ten Commandments, *"You shall have no other gods but me,"* designates that there is a power and purpose that gives life. In this sense there can only be one god. The worship of other gods separates us from what alone gives life. For the Israelites other gods were most often nature gods, local or otherwise, that were believed to have power to insure fertility, prosperity, and security. For us, these gods are less likely to be personalized but named impersonally as sex, money, and power.

The second, third, and fourth commandments detail what it is to abide in relationship with God. *We are not to "make any graven images and worship them." We are not to "take the name of God in vain." And we are to "keep holy the Sabbath."* The last six commandments specify what is correspondingly demanded in our relationships one to another. In this sense, the first four commandments are religious commands, and the last six commandments are moral commands. *We are to honor our father and mother; murder no one; be faithful in marriage;*

---

11. Irving Singer, *The Nature of Love. Vol. 1: Plato to Luther,* 2nd ed. (Chicago: University of Chicago Press, 1984), pp. 233-67.

and *neither steal nor lie.* These five commandments specify what is to be done in order for persons to be in communion with others by acknowledging and respecting them as persons. The Ten Commandments conclude with the command, *"You shall not covet."* This last command is distinct in being directed to the heart rather than against a particular act. The command is that we not seek to secure ourselves, either in immediate pleasures or in power over others. Life instead is given in a covenant in which we honor and care for others.

Christian communities inevitably move from these general commands to more particular prescriptions. As commands move to specific judgments about what should be done, they reflect particular understandings from the culture and in this sense are relative to the culture. To command persons "to honor mother and father" is to express the ends of respect and care. To command sons, however, to take on their father's profession unless released by the father's permission is relative to a particular social and familial arrangement. To command persons to "do no murder" is to express the absolute value of all people. To command persons either to remove or not to remove a dying person from life support systems, such as a respirator, is a particular judgment on the nature of the human life we value.

What is most important in understanding Christian faith and life, however, is not the development of specific moral demands and the attempt to resolve moral questions; rather, the moral law must be placed in the larger context of our relationship with God — the focus of the first four of the Ten Commandments. The fourth commandment is itself the hinge on which turns the development of the life of faith. The life of faith develops because in the worship of God relationship with God is established and deepened.

As God rested on the seventh day of creation, the Israelites are commanded to rest and not to work on the last day of the week, from sundown on Friday to sundown on Saturday. This includes remembering and celebrating the history of their relationship with God in the reading of Torah. In rest and worship they are reminded of and brought to experience the blessing of life, which is not something they achieve but something created before them and given as the gift of life itself. As for our Jewish forebears, so for Christians, Sabbath celebrates that life is given in God. The symbolism, though, is different. For Christians, the celebration of the risen Lord ends Sabbath observances in a strict sense of rest on the seventh day of the week. Instead, Sunday celebrates the fact that life is given each day in the act of offering one's life to God in thanksgiving.[12] This is the life revealed in Jesus' life and teaching, fulfilled in the Last Supper, in his passion and death, and confirmed in the resurrection. Sunday is thus the day of resurrection, the beginning of new life, "the eighth day," the first day of new life celebrated as the first day of the week. This symbolism, centered on Sunday as the first day of the week, is largely unknown in contemporary Western culture but is reflected in the format of most calendars that begin the week with Sunday and not with Monday.

For both Jew and Christian the commandment to keep holy the Sabbath is a declaration of what is central to a holy life. In this fourth commandment the first three commandments are fulfilled: God is honored as all of life is placed in relationship to God. The life that is reconciled and redeemed is grounded in the nature of things and is not a matter of moral achievement. For this reason keeping the Sabbath is a matter of worship, again not as law but as the acknowledgment, enjoyment, and deepening of God's presence in our lives. In turn, worship is the hinge that connects the first three commandments — to love God — to the last six commandments about loving the neighbor.

The Ten Commandments themselves, however, do not constitute a Christian ethic. They state the basic claim of Christian faith and the moral life, that the Christian life is a moral life grounded religiously, given in worship. The last six commandments detail basic, moral obligations between persons. They do not, though, offer an account of how we come to know and do what is good and right. In turn, the first four commandments prohibit idolatry and call for keeping the Sabbath holy. But these commands do not indicate what is the nature of true worship and, more broadly, what is the nature of the relation-

---

12. See Kathryn Greene-McCreight, "Restless Until We Rest in God," *Ex Auditu* 11 (1995): 29-41. For recent discussion of the origins and meaning of the Christian Sabbath see D. A. Carson, ed., *From Sabbath to Lord's Day: A Biblical, Historical, and Theological Investigation* (Grand Rapids: Zondervan, 1982).

ship with God given in worship or how this grounds and enables the moral life. In short, the Ten Commandments command the love of God and the love of neighbor but do not develop the nature of these loves or how the two are related. The Christian tradition may be understood as the attempt to answer these questions.

For the first thousand years in the life of the church, understandings of the Ten Commandments were offered mainly through sermons, which were in large part biblical commentaries. Alongside preaching, other writings offered accounts of particular aspects of the Christian life. For example, in the fourth century Augustine wrote about the nature of love, about the nature of the good and the nature of evil as idolatry, about freedom and the knowledge of God, and about practical matters such as marriage, political obligation, and the use of force. Together, the broad-ranging explorations of Augustine contain the elements of a systematic account of the Christian life. In Western Christianity these elements were later developed in different ways by Roman Catholics and Protestants. A comparison of these two strains of Christian ethics, Roman Catholic and Protestant, provides the opportunity to identify what are common claims central to understanding Christian faith and the moral life.[13]

Roman Catholic and Protestant Perspectives

In the thirteenth century all Catholics were required to make a confession of sin to a priest at least once a year. The confession of sin soon became a weekly obligation. The priest as confessor was responsible to declare God's forgiveness of sin and to offer pastoral support in the amendment and renewal of life.[14] In order to provide moral judgment regarding sin and pastoral guidance in light of sin, the Roman Catho-

13. See James M. Gustafson, *Protestant and Roman Catholic Ethics* (Chicago: University of Chicago Press, 1978) for an account of the similarities and differences between the two.

14. Charles Curran, "The Sacrament of Penance Today," in *Contemporary Problems in Moral Theology* (Notre Dame: Fides, 1970), pp. 1-96.

lic Church developed moral theologies. Judgments and counsel often became mechanical, in part from the sheer number of confessions heard each week. The purpose of the confession, however, was to enable persons to name those actions and attitudes that separated them from God, from their neighbor, and from themselves. To name sin was to identify what was contrary to a person's deepest desire and true identity. The naming of sin was, therefore, pastoral, to bring people back into relationship with God and with their neighbor. Where there was sorrow for sin there was forgiveness, the release from guilt, and the reestablishment of the bonds that give life wholeness. As priest, the confessor thus declared to the penitent absolution, the forgiveness of sins. Again, while confessions often devolved into mechanical judgments of sin and absolution, the deeper purpose was reconciliation.

In order to offer direction to confessors, moral theologies developed an understanding of moral responsibility and sinful acts. Often written as a separate volume called general moral theology, the first focus of moral theology was on what has been called "moral agency." The concern was how persons come to know and do the good, how mind and will are perfected or corrupted in the actions that form their lives. A second volume of moral theology then focused on what a person should do. Often called special moral theology, this volume addressed specific cases and sought to offer practical moral judgments in order to determine sinful acts.[15]

The general Roman Catholic account of the Christian moral life began with a description of the purpose or end of human life as being in relationship to God. In the end the person was to "see God." Called the beatific vision, this visual image drew together experience and purpose. The end of life was to live in the presence of God. Such a presence was to share in the mind of God. That is to say, to be in the presence of God is to be drawn into God's purpose or work. In terms of content, this end is called "blessedness." Happiness is not a matter of individual pleasure but a matter of sharing in what is ultimately good

15. For an example of a traditional moral theology, see Thomas Slater, *A Manual of Moral Theology for English-Speaking Countries,* 3rd ed. (New York: Benziger, 1908).

and purposeful. Persons can rest in this relationship because nothing is wanting. They are content and at peace, filled with a sense of glory, joy, praise, and thankfulness.

Following a discussion of the end of life, general moral theologies describe the human person in terms of virtues and vices. Virtues and vices are moral terms for describing the perfection or corruption of human powers and capacities. In matters of value, as in all matters of life, we become what we do. As such, virtues are good moral habits. Vices are bad moral habits. As developed in the ancient Greek philosophies of Plato and Aristotle, the basic human virtues are called temperance, courage, practical wisdom, and justice. These virtues were called cardinal virtues, from the Latin *cardo,* meaning "hinge," because they were understood as pivotal to human fulfillment.

Perfecting of the body is a matter of temperance, of forming bodily pleasure in right proportion so that one seeks neither excessive consumption nor excessive denial. A healthy person eats and enjoys eating. He or she is neither anorexic nor obese. The perfection of the will was a matter of the development of courage or, from the Latin translation of the Greek word for courage, also called fortitude. A person of courage is steadfast, able to act in the face of danger without becoming foolish or reckless. With fortitude a nurse is able to serve those with highly contagious diseases, taking appropriate caution, masking and gloving. Perfection of mind is a matter of practical wisdom or, from the Latin translation of the Greek, prudence. Prudence is knowing when to do what, gained through practical experience. A farmer with prudence knows when to plant and when to wait until the ground can be plowed.

As this suggests, temperance, fortitude, and prudence complement one another. For example, the young lack the experience necessary to be wise and therefore are more often foolish and intemperate. In turn, a hangover from partying into the morning hours provides knowledge more vivid than admonitions to drink in moderation. The moral life in this sense involves a harmony, a balancing of activities in order to create wholeness to life. Justice is then the last of the cardinal virtues: to give each what is appropriately due. As such, justice is a political virtue focusing on what is needed to form a community of people. Again, these excellences were understood as habits. By doing what was good, a person came to experience the good in his or her heart. Once known, the good was done naturally, almost spontaneously.

At the heart of virtue is knowledge of the good. Roman Catholic moral theology understood that such knowledge was not given simply in "growing up," or in other terms, given naturally. Instead, to know the good ultimately was a matter of the experience of God. The experience of God, in turn, formed the self. Again, the powers or capacities of the self were perfected. This ultimate — or what was called supernatural perfection — comes from God. The specific virtues were, therefore, called the theological virtues: faith, hope, and love.

Faith, as a virtue, refers both to the knowledge of God and to the act of knowing God. The experience of God was a matter of both knowledge of God and trust in God. Hope refers to the will. Instead of anxiety and despair, cynicism or bitterness, the experience of God instills hope as an openness to the future and an expectation of new opportunities and joys. Finally, love as a theological virtue refers to the experience of God as a matter of being loved. As with faith and hope, love does not simply develop from a life lived. Instead, love first comes to the Christian. As Christians have expressed this, God first loves us.

These three theological virtues are integrally related. There is no knowledge of God except knowledge born in relationship to God. Faith arises from the experience of being loved; hence faith is a matter of love. In turn, love is not simply a feeling but is a relationship to what is ultimately good. Love is grounded in what is trustworthy. Love is a matter of faith. Hope also is grounded in faith and love, just as there is no faith and love apart from hope. Together, faith, hope, and love give expression to the experience of God as acting upon us and changing us. As such they are virtues. They perfect the human power and capacity to act. Because they first arise from the experience of God as acting upon us, they are called *supernatural* virtues. They do not arise from making sense of life in general or from human effort and achievement. They are not in this sense ideals to be achieved. Instead, they are gifts from God. They are not matters of human work but matters of divine grace. As such, they come from the concrete experience of God that forms Christians in relationship to God. Central to this formation is worship and specifically the Eucharist.

Protestant thinkers shared Roman Catholic understandings that the moral life was given in the grace of God. They also emphasized the centrality of worship. What they rejected was what they judged as a narrow focus on human action. While Roman Catholic accounts of Christian faith and the moral life began with an emphasis on grace, the focus of moral theology emphasized the criteria by which to assess the goodness of human action and make judgments regarding specific cases. Protestants saw in this focus — even more so in this practice than in the written texts themselves — an undue emphasis on individual guilt and on the religious acts that should be undertaken as a remedy to sin. As Martin Luther concluded from his experience as a Roman Catholic monk, this focus on sinful acts and religious duties led to a preoccupation with oneself instead of leading to the new world of grace revealed in Jesus Christ.

The problem Protestants confronted was the opposite of that confronted by Roman Catholics. Roman Catholic moral theology developed in order to provide understanding and guidance for confessors. The problem was in naming sins and determining what to do in order to live more fully in relationship with God. The problem for Protestants was hearing the gospel. If the good news of the gospel could be heard, then there would be faith, hope, and love. The moral life would follow.

In order to hear the gospel, Protestant thinkers such as Martin Luther and John Calvin rejected the Roman Catholic framework of moral theology. The shape of the moral life was still expressed by the Ten Commandments. But what was most important was accepting that we are accepted and brought into relationship to God, apart from our own effort and work.[16] In the language of Paul, the law is good, but a person is not justified by the law. The law details acts that should and should not be done. To live by the law, according to Paul, is to focus on our acts as means to an end, for example, to avoid punishment

16. See, e.g., Martin Luther, "Lectures on Galatians," *Luther's Works,* vols. 26-27, trans. Jaroslav Pelikan (St. Louis: Concordia Publishing, 1963, 1964).

or loss or to gain favor or some other end. I tell the truth about what I am selling because if I don't and am caught I will be unable to do business. I tell the truth because it is good for business; it is more profitable. In contrast, to live by faith is to see the law as expressing the shape of the relations that are good.

The motivation to act morally comes not from the law but from the relationship that gives rise to the law in the first place. I tell the truth because I am bound to other persons; I care about them and would not want to deceive them. In this sense, law expresses and deepens the relationship that is already given. The law is like a kiss or an embrace. The kiss and the embrace express and deepen the love that is already present. Twentieth-century theologian Karl Barth expressed this understanding of law by saying "law is the form of the gospel."[17] Faith as knowledge and relationship with God is the basis of the moral life. Faith fills the heart with the love and desire to abide in and deepen the relationship with God. In this sense the Christian moral life is a matter of grace. The heart of Christian faith and life is justification by grace through faith.

Again, Protestant thinkers shared with Roman Catholics the understanding that Christian faith was a matter of radical grace, a transformation of heart and mind in terms of personal knowledge of God which resulted in new dispositions. Instead of the language of virtue as habits of perfection, however, Protestants were more likely to speak of this new life in terms of the fruit of the Holy Spirit — as joy, peace, patience, kindness, generosity, faithfulness, gentleness, and self-control (Gal. 5:22-23). The life itself was always a matter of freedom and love. The new life was freely done. Works flowed freely from the change effected by God's grace. These works were works of love, so much so that Luther could emphasize that faith is nothing but "faith active in love" (Gal. 5:6).[18]

This Protestant understanding of human life and of divine grace

17. Karl Barth, "Gospel and Law," *Community, State and Church,* trans. Will Herberg (Gloucester, Mass.: Peter Smith, 1968), pp. 71-100.

18. Martin Luther, "The Freedom of a Christian," *Luther's Works,* vol. 31, trans. Harold J. Grimm (Philadelphia: Fortress, 1957), p. 365.

is more narrowly theological than Roman Catholic understandings. Instead of focusing on the power and capacities of the human self, the focus of Christian ethics is on relationship with God. This is illustrated by the understanding of the Ten Commandments. For Protestants the primary purpose of the Ten Commandments and law in general was twofold: to describe the shape of the Christian life and to convict us of our inability to live that life on our own. For this reason, in *The Large Catechism* Luther implores all Christians to read and meditate on the Ten Commandments every day along with the Apostles' Creed and the Lord's Prayer.[19] The good designated in the Ten Commandments is never fully realized. The more that the Christian studies the law the more he or she realizes that what good there is comes from God. Only by the grace of God is given the love of God and neighbor.

For Protestants what is most important for the Christian moral life is preaching and teaching of law and gospel. Roman Catholic accounts of growth in faith and love were, at best, misplaced because they focused attention on what to do — the law — rather than on what has been done — the gospel. Despite these differences, Roman Catholic and Protestant understandings of the moral life share common convictions expressed in the Ten Commandments. As stated in the first commandment against idolatry, there is one God who is the power and meaning of all of life. To use more theological language, God is the creator and redeemer of all of life. This is what is meant in saying, "I believe in one God." The world and specifically the relationships that form our lives are of one piece. The goods of life are related, and express a unity and purpose beyond themselves. They are not randomly related. Christian faith is thus a moral life. All things are related and ordered in relationship to God. More specifically, love of God and love of neighbor are inseparable. This requires the worship of God, the acknowledgment of God, and the "resting" in God. This is the point of the fourth commandment: to keep holy the Sabbath.

19. Martin Luther, *The Large Catechism*, tr. Robert H. Fischer (Philadelphia: Fortress, 1959), p. 5.

Monotheism is the central common conviction shared by Christians. This conviction is tied to two others. The problem of human life is human sinfulness, not defined narrowly as a matter of wrong acts, but as idolatry. Understood in the context of worship, idolatry is a matter of misplaced love. Christian faith is not first of all a matter of right belief but of right relationship. In this sense, Christians share the conviction that faith is covenantal, given in a relationship with God. This covenant, moreover, is understood as a matter of grace. Grace is a matter of being loved by God, of being forgiven, of being embraced and invited into a new life. Monotheism, sin as idolatry, faith as covenantal — these are three basic beliefs Christians share in common.

Two more specific convictions Christians also share in common. Christians are Christian because they have come into the covenant with God through Jesus Christ. Jesus is, in this sense, the revelation of God. In other words, as Christians experience Jesus, Jesus is the redeemer. The knowledge of Jesus is given in scripture and worship, what Christians refer to as Word and sacrament. In scripture the story of Jesus is told as the story of God's relationship to us. In worship that relationship is acknowledged and deepened.

These common convictions about Christian faith and the moral life have not always been apparent given the polemical relationship between Roman Catholicism and Protestantism. From the sixteenth century onward, Roman Catholics and Protestants each sought to establish themselves as the religion of the individual nations of Europe and then with colonial expansion as the religion of new lands and peoples throughout the world. In this context, Roman Catholics and Protestants defined themselves over and against each other. This led to dogmatic understandings that hardened differences in terms of basic beliefs rather than fostering common understandings of Christian faith as a way of life given in response to God.

Faith came to be defined for Protestants in terms of justification by faith. Correspondingly, the absolute sovereignty of God was emphasized, so much so that predestination and double predestination were central beliefs for many Calvinists. In God's absolute power and wisdom, God knew from the beginning of time who was saved and who was damned. These beliefs were reinforced as they were conceived as the alternative to Roman Catholic "works" righteousness, in which God was reduced to a good that humans acquired. For Roman Catholics, such Protestant understandings of faith reflected an individualism centered in a subjective experience of faith. The truths of faith were denied, especially the Roman Catholic beliefs about the church and its authority. Among these defining beliefs of Roman Catholicism was the belief in the pope as head of the church, a belief that eventually was defined in terms of papal infallibility in teaching doctrine essential to faith. For Protestants, these beliefs were idolatrous in that they substituted belief in the church and the pope for faith in God.

The competition between Roman Catholicism and Protestantism fed polemics and hardened understandings of faith as a matter of mutually exclusive beliefs. Points of common identity were lost from view. Alternative frameworks that placed their different beliefs in some larger context were largely inconceivable. All of this changed only recently. While several events mark this change, none is greater than the Roman Catholic Vatican II Council that met from 1962 to 1965. Under the leadership of Pope John XXIII, this Council produced a broad range of documents that no longer defined Christian faith as Roman Catholic over and against Protestantism. Instead began the exploration of what is the faith that is shared among "all people of good will."[20]

The present age is ecumenical. Beyond polemics Roman Catholics and Protestants have sought to understand what experiences have given rise to their differences. This has led to an explosion of historical studies examining, for example, scripture, the church, worship and liturgy, theology, and ethics.[21] Thicker descriptions have been offered of the life of faith communities. Beliefs have been contextualized, placed in the broader context of these faith communities. Understandings of

20. See *Documents of Vatican II*, trans. Walter M. Abbott (New York: American Press, 1966), p. 3.
21. See Lisa Sowle Cahill and James F. Childress, eds., *Christian Ethics: Problems and Prospects* (Cleveland: Pilgrim, 1996), especially pp. 3-182.

Christian faith and life have then been enlarged by the inclusion of different communities within Roman Catholicism and Protestantism — for example, communities of women beginning in the early church and continuing through contemporary feminist and womanist movements.[22] Increasingly, other voices representing other communities of faith have also become part of this exploration of the nature of faith. For example, Eastern Orthodoxy, Anglicanism, and the Anabaptists have become important conversation partners, as well as contemporary voices ranging from new evangelical and charismatic communities to those based on liberation theologies.[23]

From each of these communities of faith come theologies that seek to offer a richly detailed description of Christian faith and the moral life. The particularity of these theologies offers the promise of an account that will do more than identify common convictions of faith. A thick description holds the promise of providing a fuller understanding of the specific features of Christian faith as a way of life. The challenge and difficulty in developing such an account is in discerning and describing these features in such a way that they represent more than ritual notes or an ethnographic description of a particular people. Instead, if such an account is to reflect the broader claims of Christian faith, it must place a particular community and tradition in the larger context of human life in general as lived in the presence of God.

This introduction to the Christian moral life is broadly Christian and particularly Anglican. In this chapter I have sought to identify the central claims regarding the nature of Christian faith and the moral life as reflected in the Ten Commandments and in the central claims of Roman Catholics and Protestants. In the next chapter I will turn from defining beliefs about the nature of Christian faith and life to a

22. See, e.g., Charles E. Curran, Margaret A. Farley, and Richard A. McCormick, eds., *Feminist Ethics and the Catholic Moral Tradition. Moral Theology 9* (New York: Paulist, 1996).

23. For an introduction to contemporary voices in theology, see Roger Badham, ed., *Introduction to Christian Theology: Contemporary North American Perspectives* (Louisville, Ky.: Westminster/John Knox, 1998).

more detailed description of this life as lived, given my experience and understanding of faith as formed by the Anglican tradition. These first two chapters provide something of a bifocal vision in order to offer in the remaining chapters a thicker, more detailed account of Christian faith as a way of life grounded in the worship of God.

[CHAPTER 2]

An Anglican Perspective

∿

I WAS BORN into the Episcopal Church. My earliest memories were at ages four and five. My parents lived in a one-bedroom apartment, a fortunate find at the end of World War II when housing was limited. Two small boys meant no automobile. We walked the mile plus to the English Victorian-style church with dark wood pews and beams. The stained glass diffused what light there was. But from the light outside and the candles inside, the vaulted space was ethereal. We kneeled, sat, and stood in line — parents, sons, and my very English paternal grandmother. The world was filled with the spirit or spirits of God. God simply was in the fabric of things — just there, like my grandmother in her silent prayers.

We moved, my grandmother died, and there were different churches, some with, some without the colored glass and the vaulted space. But week-in and week-out, with some periods of exception, we went to church and listened to the stories of the Bible (however disconnected they were from week to week), sometimes retold in the sermon. And we regularly celebrated the Lord's Supper, receiving bread and wine as the apostles did in remembrance of Jesus' last supper, death, and resurrection. I became Christian as I grew up in the church, though this was no more a natural process then is the learning of a language. I actually became Christian as the stories I heard became my story, as they made sense of life as I knew it and as I lived it — the command of the prophets to do justice, the lament of the psalms, the call to forgive, the promise of forgiveness and new life. The themes that construed my life were themselves always framed more broadly by the story of Jesus — his life, ministry, death, and resurrection.

My Christian faith was quite simply a way of life formed in a community of faith. This faith born from the church has matured in the church as well, for 20 years now in the daily worship and life of a seminary community. This has meant quiet meditation, listening to scripture, common prayer, and often Eucharist together. My family joined me regularly, often followed by a community meal. Worship thus framed our life together. To the outside observer, this may have seemed self-contained. This life, however, always reached out beyond ourselves. We were members of communities: schools, work, towns and cities, professional associations, civic organizations, recreation groups. Visitors were welcomed. And always people were going out to live and serve in the world beyond the seminary.

I share these autobiographical reflections because they indicate something of my own situation, of how I am situated in particular communities within the Episcopal Church as part of the larger Anglican Communion. My experience has been shaped by this history so that I experience and understand Christian faith indelibly as an Anglican Christian. This means that I wear bifocal glasses as I come to write this account of the Christian moral life. As with all Christian ethics, this ethic is informed by a larger look at the Christian tradition that has formed me. This longer look begins with scripture and continues with the witness of Christians, from the witness of early Christian communities to that of specific thinkers, especially those who have formed the Catholic and Protestant traditions in the West. The shorter look is Anglican, moving in the other direction from my own experience in the Episcopal Church outward to Anglican thinkers who have developed their own accounts of Christian faith and life.

These two focal points, the one near and the other farther from my experience, provide contrast in my vision. My Anglican perspective informs my seeing what is true in Roman Catholic and Protestant traditions. In turn, the central claims of these two major traditions of Western Christianity inform my understanding of what is the faith I have received from within the Anglican tradition. The hope is that the more particular experiences and understandings of faith and the more universal claims about the nature of faith will be brought together so that they illumine one another.

The conclusions of the last chapter were fivefold. Christian faith is monotheistic and covenantal. Sin is idolatry. The covenant with God is revealed and effected in Jesus Christ. This relationship is begun and deepened in scripture and worship. Anglicans share these convictions. However, in contrast to Roman Catholic and Protestant thought, what is most distinctive about Anglicanism is that the English Church sought to allow for greater differences in understanding of these convictions than either Protestant churches or the Roman Catholic Church.

Given the adversarial relationship with Roman Catholicism, Protestant traditions were initially confessional. For example, Lutherans defined their faith in the Augsburg Confession; the Calvinists defined theirs in the Westminster Confession. These confessions offered definitions of faith in opposition to the particular beliefs or dogma required by the Roman Catholic Church. As a nation of Catholics and Protestants, England instead developed a distinctive tradition in which faith was identified more with faithful worship that bound a people together in a holy life than with the confession of beliefs.[1] In this sense, Anglicanism has more clearly identified Christian faith as a matter of practical piety.

As a matter of practical piety, Christian convictions are expressed in Anglicanism more in terms of relationships than as matters of belief about God, Jesus Christ, and the Holy Spirit — especially the authority of scripture and of the church in matters of right belief. First, Anglicans understand Christian faith as incarnational. Grounded in convictions of monotheism, faith is experienced in all the relations of our

---

1. For a good introduction to Anglicanism, its history, worship, and theology, see Stephen Sykes and John Booty, eds., *The Study of Anglicanism* (London and Philadelphia: SPCK/Fortress, 1988).

lives and not apart from them. In this sense, God is incarnational, literally enfleshed in the world in which we live. God is not "spirit" apart from the world. Instead, God is the meaning and power that creates and redeems life itself. Anglican theologian and Archbishop of Canterbury William Temple expressed this incarnational understanding by saying that Christianity is the most materialist of the world religions and, at the same time, that the incarnation is not some form of crude materialism.[2] To say that God is incarnate is to say that the meaning and power that is the source of life is given in this world but is not reducible to the material world or to the human body with its passions and pleasures.

Second, the covenantal character of Christian faith is reflected in an Anglican understanding of piety as corporate. The relationship or bond that gives wholeness to life brings the individual into relationship with all of life. The life formed in faith is never individual. It is always a life formed in community in order to become a holy people. This second conviction may be called the corporateness of faith. Faith as piety is corporate, to be a people — what Christians call the people of God.

Third, an Anglican understanding of Christian piety is sacramental. Incarnate, the covenant with God is revealed and deepened through what are variously called signs, symbols, and sacraments. Thirteenth-century Roman Catholic theologian Thomas Aquinas defined sacrament as that which effects what it signifies.[3] For example, a kiss or an embrace points to love and shares in the deepening creation of that love. A kiss signifies love and, in turn, creates as it deepens that love. For Christians, knowledge and relationship with God are given fully and sufficiently in scripture and worship. As sacrament, the authority of Word and sacrament is not in revealing or stating right belief but in drawing the Christian more deeply into relationship with God.

2. William Temple, *Nature, Man, and God* (London: Macmillan, 1934), p. 478.

3. See Karl Rahner, "Introductory Observations on Thomas Aquinas' Theology of the Sacraments in General," *Theological Investigations,* vol. 14 (London: Darton, Longman, & Todd, 1976), pp. 149-60.

More specifically, Jesus is the sacrament of God.[4] Jesus reveals the nature of God. Those who acknowledge Jesus are then brought into a new or deeper relationship with God. What Jesus reveals he effects. In following Jesus, Christians become the people of God. As such they form the church, which is the sacrament of Christ in the world.

Altogether, Christian faith is a practical piety that is corporate, incarnate, and sacramental. These three characteristics of practical piety are integrally related. Practical piety as a way of life is what is meant by discipleship. This way of life is never individual. To be formed in God is to love one another. Such a faith is never individualistic but always corporate. Corporate Christian faith is incarnate; God is in the very fabric of things. To relate to the pattern in this life there must be something to reveal the pattern. For Christians, Jesus is this revelation. As such he is the sacrament of God, drawing us into the practical piety of faith. As a way of life, Christians in turn become the sacrament of Christ to the world.

Faith as a Way of Life

In English Christianity, faith as a way of life always has an intimate quality to it. The church was experienced and understood as tied to the village or neighborhood. Religion was not an austere authority from afar, as Rome and the pope came to be for many Catholics as well as Protestants. Nor was the church viewed as realized more fully in the "religious," in the male and female monastic communities set aside from the world for a life of prayer. Instead, Anglicanism came to see Christian faith from the perspective of fairly small communities whose life was gathered up, celebrated, and formed through common worship. The circumstances of England and of the English Reformation made this possible.

The break with Rome closed the monasteries in 1536, but a Benedictine spirituality remained integral to Anglicanism. Benedictine

4. Edward Schillebeeckx, *Christ the Sacrament of the Encounter with God,* trans. Paul Barrett (New York: Sheed & Ward, 1963).

communities had been central to religion in England.[5] There in these communities daily life had been formed around what were called the disciplines of prayer, study, and work. Each day was structured around a *lectio divina,* a set of offices of worship centered in the reading of scripture, saying the Psalms, and offering common prayer. Gathering together seven times a day, the monks would begin with matins or morning prayer before sunrise and end with compline at the end or completion of the day. Worship punctuated the day with a rhythm so that prayer, study, and work formed a harmonic chord.

Prayer was not separate from daily life but the celebration and offering of all of life in God. In turn, study was not academic but meditative. Specifically, the study of scripture was a matter of standing before scripture in order to listen and experience how God has been present in the changing times of life, in the whole cycle of events from birth to death, in joy and in sorrow. Work as well was a form of prayer and study. Whether in the work of the garden or in managing community matters, work was life in God, without which prayer and study were together like a soul without a body, form without content.

Much of Benedictine spirituality was itself claimed in the Protestant vision of Christian faith as given in the daily life of a people shaped in the worship of God. The central hallmark of Protestantism was an open Bible. Scripture is the Word of God where the revelation and power effecting grace in our lives is given. This experience of God's presence given through scripture was focused in the understanding of "justification by grace through faith." These words may be most simply defined as being made just or right in relationship to God, not by our works but as simply given, as grace. This we know by faith, that is to say, in a trust in such grace that comes in hearing the Christian story. Given this fundamental conviction, the Bible was to be read in the language of the people and made avail-

5. See Bede, *A History of the English Church and People,* trans. Leo Sherley-Price (Baltimore: Penguin, 1955). Written by the Benedictine monk Bede in 731, this history offers a firsthand account of the initial development of Christianity in England and provides a picture of the central place and character of Benedictine religious communities.

able to all for study and worship. In turn, worship was common worship, a regular gathering of the people of God to hear God's Word, to acknowledge God's grace, and to offer their daily lives in God. In this larger context the Protestant protest against clericalism and emphasis on the laity and lay vocation makes sense. The presence of God's redeeming life is not in religious life separate from daily life but in our common life.

These Protestant convictions shared the deepest understanding of the forms of worship that had shaped Benedictine monastic communities. Instead of rejecting wholesale the Roman Catholic forms of worship, Thomas Cranmer created a Book of Common Prayer that appropriated Roman Catholic forms of worship reformed by sources from the early church and from the Protestant Reformation.[6] Like the monastic communities, the English Book of Common Prayer structured worship in terms of a daily office of worship. Instead of seven offices there were two, Morning and Evening Prayer. In turn, the reading of scripture was organized around a lectionary, so that with daily reading the Old Testament would be basically read once a year while the New Testament would be read every four months, the Psalms every month.[7] Here, as with the Benedictine communities, worship was a daily affair of listening to scripture and the offering of thanks and prayers for "our daily bread" and that of the world.

The Book of Common Prayer also reformed the Eucharist so that it was the celebration of the community in its life given in Christ.[8] In Holy Eucharist the worshiping community offers its life, individually and together, to God. This is a matter of commendation. As the

6. For the most recent, comprehensive account of Cranmer, see Diarmid MacCulloch, *Thomas Cranmer: A Life* (New Haven, Conn.: Yale University Press, 1996).

7. For an understanding of the history of the creation of the Book of Common Prayer, see Marion J. Hatchett, "Prayer Books," in *The Study of Anglicanism*, pp. 121-33.

8. See William Crockett, *Eucharist: Symbol of Transformation* (New York: Pueblo, 1989), pp. 164-80.

life of Jesus reaches its culmination in his commendation of himself to God, in his crucifixion and death, Jesus represents and presents to us life lived in relationship to God. The Eucharist is hence Holy Communion: dying with Christ, the worshiper is raised into relationship with God. In the Book of Common Prayer, the concern was in enabling participation in this worship and not, as Richard Hooker emphasized, in "the manner how."[9]

It is easy to create a romantic picture of Anglican worship. No doubt the reality of worship was often far removed from this vision of forming a holy and godly people, what I have called a practical piety grounded in the worship of God. However, the Book of Common Prayer offered a point of reference, in the book itself and in its use as the worship required by law as the public worship in England. Christian faith was a corporate, practical piety that understood the Christian life sacramentally and incarnationally. Faith is enfleshed in our daily lives. The Christian life is a matter of holiness, of living in and deepening the experience of God's presence in our lives together. This we know and do in Christ.

Something of this ideal of an Anglican vision of Christian faith is expressed in George Herbert's seventeenth-century classic, *The Country Parson*.[10] The church stood at the center of village life. On Sunday mornings the community gathered together in worship to offer to God their lives together. And what they did on Sundays was re-created every day. In the morning and evening while they worked in the fields, shops, and homes, the church bell would ring. They knew that the priest, with perhaps a few others, would be celebrating the offices of Morning and Evening Prayer. In this way they knew that their lives

9. Richard Hooker, *Of the Lawes of Ecclesiastical Politie*. Folger Library Edition, ed. Speed Hill (Cambridge, Mass.: Harvard University Press, 1977-1981), vol. 5, bk. 67, sec. 3. The text is available at a more modest cost by a reprinting of the 1887 edition edited by John Keble. Richard Hooker, *Of the Laws of Ecclesiastical Polity,* 3 vols. (Ellicott City, Md.: Via Media, 1994). On participation see also Crockett, pp. 176-80.

10. John N. Wall, Jr., ed., *George Herbert: The Country Parson, The Temple. The Classics of Western Spirituality* (New York: Paulist Press, 1981), pp. 54-115.

were held in the daily round of prayer. This was made possible because the parson was a daily part of their lives. He knew them and celebrated with them times of joy and times of sorrow. They were the church, and he was their pastor.

English Christianity and its heirs, the Anglican and Episcopal churches throughout the world, have at their best offered this vision of Christian faith as a matter of practical piety without confusing faith with right belief. In large measure this is the result of necessity.[11] The Protestant Reformation of the sixteenth and seventeenth centuries threatened any peace as Protestant churches sought independence from the established religion of Roman Catholicism. The peace and unity of England, like those of its neighbors on the continent, were threatened. The break with Rome following Henry VIII's annulment in 1533 left England with the question of religious alignment. The monarchy succeeding Henry VIII, that of Edward, turned towards Protestantism. In turn, his successor, Queen Mary, repealed the legislation of Edward and pressed for a Roman Catholic nation.

It is almost impossible for us now to comprehend the conflicts over religious faith in this period of time. This is because religious faith was viewed as essential to the life of a nation. That is why one church was established by the state. Religious faith bound individuals together in interlocking sets of duties and responsibilities. Relationships were formed that extended civility, respect, and accountability in order to establish a commonwealth — literally, something of worth shared in common. A nation depended on the establishment of one religion. Religion was the soul of the nation.

The conflict between Protestantism and Roman Catholicism was not simply a matter of religious beliefs but of the details of religious life. During the monarchy of King Edward, Protestants destroyed the stone altars and images that had adorned the churches. The celebration of holy days when particular saints were remembered and venerated was prohibited, as were the use of vestments and many symbolic actions such as making the sign of the cross or kneeling and bowing at

11. See Timothy F. Sedgwick, "The New Shape of Anglican Identity," *Anglican Theological Review* 77 (Spring 1995): 187-97.

the name of Jesus. These changes were accomplished by dismissing priests and bishops who opposed such changes and in their place appointing new, more Protestant leaders. What was done under Edward was undone by Mary, beginning with returning the more Catholic bishops to power so that they could in turn remove clergy who opposed the return to more Catholic ways. Again, these conflicts were seen as a matter of fighting for the soul of the nation. As such, Protestant reformers who did not seek sanctuary in France or some other country outside of England were imprisoned. Some were executed, including Thomas Cranmer, who had been the primary author of the first English Book of Common Prayer.

Threatened by unending civil war, the next monarch, Queen Elizabeth I (ruled 1558-1603) sought some middle ground between Protestantism and Roman Catholicism. In what is called the "Elizabethan Settlement," she set the grounds for the establishment of English Christianity. England was to establish the church but as neither Protestant nor Roman Catholic. Although England was in fact thrown into civil war following Elizabeth's immediate successors, at the end of that war the English Christianity of Queen Elizabeth was established. At the heart of this form of Christian faith was common worship as given in the Book of Common Prayer. A common practice of faith was established that reflected a compromise or middle way (a *via media*) between Protestantism and Roman Catholicism. Differences in understanding that threatened common worship were acknowledged and in large measure respected. These differences were many, ranging from the most purely theological understandings of the nature of God to understandings of how God is present in worship. The understanding of Christian faith itself centered then not on right beliefs but on right worship, in order to form a people in relationship with God. In this sense, Christian faith is a practical piety that is corporate, incarnate, and sacramental. This is evident in the range of different Anglican works in theology.

The Theological Tradition

In the developing course of its history, Anglican theologians have of-fered a variety of defenses of Anglicanism.[12] By defense I mean they have sought an account of Christian faith and life that made sense of the Church of England. Richard Hooker (1554-1600) wrote the first of these accounts during the rule of Queen Elizabeth. Written as seven books and called *The Laws of Ecclesiastical Polity,* Hooker began by claiming that the nature of God is like that of law.

By law, Hooker did not have in mind the law narrowly under-stood as command and obedience. Instead, law referred more broadly to the nature of things. To say "the being of God is a kind of law to God's working"[13] is to say that God is the power that permeates or grounds all of life, that this power is good and that this power is pur-poseful. This is what is meant by saying that Christian faith is incarnational. We express this personally by saying God creates, sus-tains, and redeems life. This purposefulness, moreover, is not nar-rowly human. All things serve a larger purpose. As God is the purpose that is in life and draws life forward into the future, it makes sense to say that all of life is in God and serves God. This end is ultimately be-yond human comprehension. All that we can say reflects our particu-lar and limited perceptions. But, Hooker claims, nonetheless, we know this goodness as we come to participate more fully in the pur-poses or in what are called "the ends" of life.

As with many theologians, Hooker indicates his sense of the ends of life through his reflections on angels. Angels are understood as spirits, like humans but without physical bodies; and they therefore intimate what human life is at its highest. What then do angels do? Hooker says simply, as they behold the face of God, "in admiration of so great excellency they all adore him; and being rapt with the love of his beauty, they cleave inseparably for ever unto him."[14] The end of life

12. See Paul Avis, "What is 'Anglicanism'?" in *The Study of Anglicanism,* pp. 405-24.

13. Hooker, I.2.2.

14. Hooker, I.4.1.

is not some calculation of individual benefit. The end of life is a glorious mystery, beyond comprehension, a beauty that is simply good. Participation in this life is a matter of love and adoration. Such love and adoration moves naturally from praise and thanksgiving to the embrace and care of the world.

Hooker goes on to argue in *The Laws* that this way of glory is revealed in scripture and known in worship. Scripture is not a book of laws that command unknowing obedience. Instead, scripture is the story of the purposes of God. Scripture is saving knowledge as it reveals and effects participation in this larger way of life. Scripture reveals God by bringing us into relationship with God, what Hooker speaks about as participation. The knowledge of God is not factual knowledge about the nature of things. Instead, to know God is to be in relationship with God, to participate in the purposes of God. For this reason, Christians cannot avoid mystical language. To know God is to share in the divine mystery, to be united to God. This involves the whole of life, drawing the individual person out from him or herself until the person no longer sees his or her life in terms of individual fulfillment. Instead, life is given corporately, in being a people, a people who in the celebration of life as given in God are drawn out to love and serve one another.

The holy life for Christians is given in practices and disciplines. Scripture points to these, but it would be a mistake to understand scripture as detailing or commanding what ought to be done in all aspects of life. Scripture is silent about many things. What it does prescribe is often a particular judgment given to an early Christian community about what is needed in order to be a people who love and adore God and so care for one another. This is the case in a wide range of areas, from Paul's instructions about whether to eat foods sacrificed to idols (1 Cor. 8:1-13) to the difference in judgments regarding the permissibility of divorce, from the prohibition in the gospels of Mark and Luke (Mark 10:2-12; Luke 16:18) to the pastoral exception allowing for divorce in the Gospel of Matthew (Matt. 5:31-32) and in Paul's counsel to the Corinthians (1 Cor. 7:10-16).[15] Prescriptions in scripture address concerns for

15. See Philip Turner, "The Marriage Canons of the Episcopal Church," *Anglican Theological Review* 65 (October 1983): 371-93 and 66 (January 1984): 1-22.

the community of faith. However, whether of matters regarding manners or morals, such judgments of scripture are not in themselves the revelation of scripture. While the judgments of the Christian community of faith need to be taken seriously, they may also for good reason be modified or finally rejected in light of the larger purpose of forming a holy people who care for one another as they direct their lives towards God. Manners and morals thus change, evolve. They are integral to faith as a holy life but not as ends in themselves.

The broader practices that express and shape the Christian life are themselves the subject of debate within the Christian community. For Anglicans, these practices cannot be derived from scripture alone, as the Protestant Puritans had maintained and whom Hooker opposed. Scripture is not a book of rules. Rather, the practices of faith, such as the forms of worship, arise in response to scripture. In turn, practices of Christian faith cannot be strictly identified with all of the customs and judgments of a particular church and community, especially where such customs and judgments were commanded as essential to faith by the church itself. On this basis Hooker rejected Roman Catholic claims of papal authority. Instead, the practices of faith can only be construed broadly in view of scripture and the worship and teaching of the early church. As expressed in the Book of Common Prayer, for Anglicans this has meant the reading of scripture, prayer and worship, table fellowship, abiding love of others, and the embrace and care of those in need outside the accepted boundaries of the community. This is what I mean by speaking of Christian faith as practical piety — what Anglicans have called a holy or godly way of life.

What makes this way of life Christian is that it is revealed and begun in Jesus. In this sense scripture and worship are integrally related. To read and listen to scripture draws the person into the worship of God. Forms of worship are, in turn, grounded in scripture. Together they enable participation in a godly life. So, for example, the sacrament of Holy Eucharist, says Hooker, does not narrowly teach the mind. Rather, it is a "heavenly ceremony" by which we participate in the end for which we are intended.[16] This conviction is so strong for

16. Hooker, I.57.3.

Hooker that the arguments between Roman Catholics and Protestants about how Christ is present in the bread and wine of the Eucharist corrupt faith by requiring belief instead of enabling participation. The important thing about the Eucharist is that there is "real participation of Christ and of life in his body and blood." This is what Christians experience and is itself the basis for their understanding and particular interpretations about what is happening. Again, Hooker concludes with the wish that all "would more give themselves to meditate with silence what we have by the sacrament, and less to dispute of the manner how."[17]

Anglican divines (a word given to designate Anglican theologians)[18] have addressed other, different questions or challenges than did Hooker. Their theologies differ in form as well as content. At the same time, they share Hooker's convictions about Christian faith. For example, following Hooker the three greatest apologists in Anglicanism are arguably Joseph Butler, Frederick Denison Maurice, and William Temple. In the eighteenth century Butler sought to make sense of Christian faith in the age of science. In a series of fifteen sermons, Butler turned from describing Christian faith in terms of the purposefulness of God as law, to describing the experience of faith, of how we come to know God, as a matter of the love of neighbor and the love of God given in worship.[19]

17. Hooker, V.67.3.

18. Obviously, the choice of Anglican divines who represent the tradition is itself an interpretation of tradition. Still, there is some consensus on these major figures in Anglicanism. See John Booty, "Standard Divines," *The Study of Anglicanism,* pp. 163-74. Booty's list includes Richard Hooker, Lancelot Andrewes, Jeremy Taylor, William Law, Joseph Butler, Charles Simeon, John Keble, Edward Pusey, John Henry Newman, Frederick Denison Maurice, Joseph Barber Lightfoot, F. J. A. Hort, Brooke Foss Westcott, Charles Gore, and William Temple. This list of divines is for Booty complemented by other, more contemporary persons such as Evelyn Underhill, Vida Scudder, C. S. Lewis, Owen Barfield, Charles Williams, Dorothy Sayers, T. S. Eliot, and William Stringfellow.

19. Joseph Butler, *Fifteen Sermons Preached at the Rolls Chapel* and *A Dissertation on the Nature of Virtue,* ed. T. A. Roberts (London: SPCK, 1970), esp. sermons 11-14.

In the nineteenth century, F. D. Maurice confronted a very different challenge to understanding Christian faith. Instead of the new sciences, Maurice addressed the question of history: "What is Christian faith given its varied historical forms and understandings?" Maurice's answer in *The Kingdom of Christ* is that faith is the life that the church in its worship celebrates and effects.[20] In the twentieth century William Temple offers yet another apology for Christian faith. In *Nature, Man, and God,* Temple argues for a personal understanding of God as the most adequate way to understand the creativity and relationships given in the process of creation.[21]

Each of these thinkers — Hooker, Taylor, Butler, Maurice, and Temple — have a different set of questions they seek to answer in order to make sense of Christian faith. They are not Anglican divines because they develop a common doctrine of belief. Rather, they seek to understand the faith that they have been given as a matter of practical piety. What they share in common is this practical piety that is incarnational, corporate, and sacramental.

Other Anglican divines have been more poets and pastors than philosophers and professors. They have not so much sought to formulate a final account of Christian belief as they have sought to explore the Christian life. Anglican tradition is not narrowly a tradition of systematic or dogmatic theology. There is no Thomas Aquinas or John Calvin. Even the more systematic works, beginning with Hooker, have been more occasional and pastoral than systematic or dogmatic. Still other writings have been devotional explorations and meditations on Christian living, for example, the poetic and literary tradition from John Donne and George Herbert to C. S. Lewis, T. S. Eliot, and R. S. Thomas. Jeremy Taylor is the exemplar of this tradition.

Following the civil war, when England rejected Anglicanism and became a Puritan state under Oliver Cromwell (from 1649-1660),

20. Frederick Denison Maurice, *The Kingdom of Christ,* 2 vols., ed. Alec R. Vidler (London: SCM, 1958). For a broader selection of writings addressing faith in light of history, see Ellen K. Wondra, ed., F. D. Maurice, *Reconstructing Christian Ethics: Selected Writings* (Louisville, Ky.: Westminster/John Knox, 1995).

21. Temple, esp. pp. 277-325.

Jeremy Taylor wrote from underground two Anglican classics that have since remained virtually in continuous print, *The Exercise of Holy Living* and *The Exercise of Holy Dying*.[22] In straightforward fashion, *Holy Living* details how the individual person should shape his or her daily life in terms of body, society, and God — what Taylor speaks of as "sobriety, justice, and religion." The focus is on the actions that form our life: "our deportment in our personal and private capacities, the fair treating of our bodies and spirits . . . our duty to all relations to our Neighbour . . . [and] the offices of direct Religion, and entercourse with God."[23] The interest is on shaping our understanding and desire. In *Holy Dying* Taylor turns then to meditations on death in order to more directly change understanding and desire, the wellspring of action. The larger purpose of these writings is characteristic of Anglican theology and ethics: to enable persons to know and to see the presence of God in all of life.

Taylor begins *Holy Dying* with the image of the human person as a bubble in a world that is itself a storm, a vapor, an appearing and disappearing. The succession of time preaches our funeral sermon. We seek refuge in bodily pleasures, material wealth, and the opinion of others. Desires multiply as if periods of pleasure could fulfill, as if quantity could somehow make something enduring. Like a narcotic, they give immediate pleasure but at the price of dulling the larger sense of things. Moreover, they demand absolute devotion. Life becomes a single-minded pursuit of these false elixirs. Life is lived in an endless rush from moment to moment. Fear of loss makes joy and peace impossible.

The knowledge of the fragility and transience of life is not itself morbid. Death, says Taylor, "is not the going out of this world, but *the manner of going*." Damnation "is called eternal death; not because it kills or ends the duration; it hath not so much good in it; but because it is a perpetual infelicity."[24] Holy dying is instead holy living. This

22. Jeremy Taylor, *Holy Living and Holy Dying*, 2 vols., ed. P. G. Stanwood (Oxford, Clarendon, 1989).
23. Taylor, *Holy Living and Holy Dying*, vol. 1, p. 60.
24. Taylor, *Holy Living and Holy Dying*, vol. 2, p. 69.

knowledge offers the only way to break hold of the bondage of worldly pleasures and social conceits. The larger arc of *Holy Dying* is eucharistic. To know that all is passing away, we are released from cleaving to ephemeral satisfactions into thanksgiving for the larger blessings of life. We rightly love natural beauty and human friendship. But they remain lovely only in receiving them and letting them go. They are gifts and not possessions. This eucharistic life — literally a life of thanksgiving — is revealed in Christ, in his dying into God and being raised into new life.

For all his brilliance as an English writer and all his erudition as a scholar, Jeremy Taylor was first of all a pastor. As George Herbert envisioned, he assumed that the church was the community in its daily life as that life was formed and celebrated in the worship of God. The purpose of the church and its ministry was to support and celebrate this life. A description of the Christian moral life was not focused narrowly on what to do, but on what should be desired in order that the presence of God may be known and deepened in all of life. As Taylor confronted the challenge of a society where worship was prohibited, his concern was how to effect the acknowledgment and worship of God. Hence his account of the Christian life is devotional. He offers meditations, prayers, and exhortations that are in form and content that of worship. In contrast to Anglican apologists who sought to give an account of Christian faith, Taylor sought to create eucharistic worship.

In addition to the apologetic and devotional character of Anglican theologies, others have developed their thought in terms of other questions, most notably questions of evangelism and ethics. John Wesley, for example, was less concerned with making sense of Christian faith in light of contemporary thought than with enabling the many poor English workers to hear the Christian story so that it could transform their lives. In religious language, Wesley was concerned with saving souls. His sermons then describe the experience of sin in terms of the brokenness of life, and describe salvation in terms of healing and new life.[25] In terms of ethics, William Wilber-

---

25. John Wesley, *John Wesley's Sermons: An Anthology,* ed. Albert C. Outler and Richard P. Heitzenrater (Nashville, Tenn.: Abingdon, 1991).

force offered prophetic writings against slavery at the end of the eighteenth century, while Kenneth Kirk sought to develop a moral theology adequate to the experience of God.[26] A whole other line of thinkers gave voice to Christian faith in terms of a Christian vision of society grounded in the worship of God.[27] However different these works are, they confirm that Anglicans share a common faith and a common understanding that faith is a matter of practical piety, given in and through the church as its life is formed in worship. The purpose of theology is not narrowly systematic but is more pastoral, in the sense of seeking to deepen the experience of the presence of God in the world about us.

What is true of English Christianity is true of Anglicanism as a world communion of churches outside of England. To "do theology" is to seek to bring people into relationship with God. The clearest contemporary example of such Anglican thought is offered in the writings of Desmond Tutu.[28] From priest to Archbishop of Cape Town, South Africa, Tutu was confronted by the violent and dehumanizing politics of apartheid. His preaching and teaching, public witness and protest were prophetic denunciations of evil and annunciations of what was intended for human community. The Christian faith born of Anglicanism was the foundation for his teaching. Liberation was not won

---

26. William Wilberforce, *A Practical View of the Prevailing Religious System of Professed Christians Contrasted with Real Christianity* (London: SCM, 1958); Kenneth Kirk, *Some Principles of Moral Theology* (London: Longmans, 1920), and *The Vision of God* (London: Longmans, 1931). See also Kirk, *Conscience and Its Problems,* with a critical introduction by David H. Smith (Louisville, Ky.: Westminster/John Knox, 1999).

27. See Maurice B. Reckitt, *Maurice to Temple: A Century of the Social Movement in the Church of England* (London: Faber & Faber, 1947); and John Oliver, *The Church and Social Order* (London: Mowbray, 1968). Among these writers see William Temple, *Christus Veritas* (London: Macmillan, 1917) and, as adapted for lectures given at Oxford in 1931, *Christian Faith and Life* (Harrisburg, Penn.: Morehouse, 1994); and V. A. Demant, *God, Man and Society* (Milwaukee, Wisc.: Morehouse, 1934).

28. The best collection of writings may be found in Desmond Tutu, *The Rainbow People of God,* ed. John Allen (New York: Doubleday, 1994).

but given in Christ. The church was to bear witness to this reality in its life. This meant solidarity with the oppressed, being with and for the people, even at the risk and price of life. Always, though, this was grounded in prayer and worship, in the celebration of this new life given in Christ. Nowhere was this incarnational vision more vivid than when Tutu would lead a public gathering of mourners for a black protester who had been killed by the apartheid government. Worship — preaching, prayer, singing — was always praise and thanksgiving for the new life that God has promised and had been given by those who had died.

Tutu's prophetic witness has always had a dual focus. On the one hand, he has addressed the injustice and oppression of the state, calling for a new order to form a new people in South Africa. On the other hand, he has called the church to be the witness and bearer of this new creation. The story of faith, of crucifixion and resurrection, is the story of liberation into becoming the people of God. This meant renouncing a narrowly defined sacred space and tradition for religion. Instead, the church must tell the story of scripture, must pray, and must sing together in order to stand in the presence of God. At the same time, this meant standing with those who protest injustice and work for a world in which all people share in a life together where each person is valued and respected. The story of faith is the story of our lives. Such is the nature of a faith that is incarnational and sacramental.

Theology and Ethics

Again, to an outsider who simply reads the variety of works of Anglicans, the range of Anglican works appears to lack a common understanding. This is so precisely because the identity of the Anglican tradition as a form of Christianity is not a matter of a confession of beliefs but a way of life that is given in the church. In this way of life, the community of Christians confronts a range of challenges and asks a range of questions. Theologies arise from within the church as attempts to address these challenges and questions. When these theologies are simply compared they appear to offer rather different understandings of Christian faith — some very Protestant, some Catholic, and some philosophical, with little concern for Jesus Christ except as a model for our behavior. Some thinkers focus on scripture and Jesus Christ as redeemer. Others turn their attention to worship and what is vaguely called the sacramental life. Others describe the nature of God, human life, and the natural world. And then there are those who focus their accounts of Christian faith on morality itself, on what should be done individually and in the world.

These theologies are never a substitute for what I have called a practical piety, an identity given in a life lived in the community of faith. Theologies do not stand alone. Again, they respond to challenges and questions. As this text is itself a theology, specifically a moral theology, it may be helpful to identify some of the different questions that give rise to the different theologies as these shape the focus of ethics. In this light I want to clarify what is needed in order to offer a unified account of the Christian life and hence the purpose of this introduction to the Christian life.

Historical theology retrieves historical texts and seeks to give voice to these texts that they may be understood theologically as explorations and expressions of Christian faith. In this sense, historical theology includes biblical studies. *Systematic theology* seeks to offer an ordered expression of faith. As systematic, such theologies are Trinitarian: they develop understandings of Christian faith as a matter of God as Father, Son, and Holy Spirit. This includes claims about the nature of God, about revelation, and about the divine activity. As such, systematic theology is closely related to philosophical theology or what Roman Catholics call fundamental theology. *Philosophical theology* gives an account of the historically determinate expressions of Christian faith in terms of other, more general accounts of the nature of things, or as William Temple says, of nature, man, and God.

Instead of focusing on common human understandings, the concern of others within the church has been on Christian beliefs themselves. *Dogmatic theology* seeks to articulate these beliefs in their interrelationships. *Evangelical theology* gives an even more particular voice to Christian faith as a matter of good news, as saving knowledge, as the action of God or the story that gives new life, what is variously called conversion, reconciliation, redemption, and eternal life.

In addition to these accounts of faith — whether historical, systematic, philosophical, dogmatic, or evangelical — more particular questions also have focused theologies. *Ascetical theology* focuses on the disciplines and practices that bring a person more deeply into relationship with God. Closely related, *mystical theology* gives an account of the developing experience of God. *Sacramental theologies* describe how Christian faith is given and passed on within the community of faith and to the world. Here the focus shifts from the mystical experience of God to the church and especially to worship and to "Word and sacrament." *Pastoral theology* turns more practically to how Christian faith is nurtured in the care of persons in the cycles and crises of life.

The actual theological writings of a tradition may be more or less systematic, more or less devotional, and more or less focused on one or more of the questions and concerns designated by each of these "types" of theology.[29] There is, in other words, no pure type of theology. Each informs and to some extent requires the answers explored and developed by the other theologies. The most comprehensive theologies variously combine different types of theology. As reflected in the work of Thomas Aquinas, Roman Catholic systematic theologies have often been heavily philosophical, making sense of Christian faith in terms of more general accounts of God and the world. In contrast, Protestant thought has emphasized how Christ and scripture are a matter of conversion. These systematic theologies have often, then, been more evangelical. When the concern is right belief, both Roman Catholic and Protestant theologies tend to become more dogmatic. Eastern Orthodoxy has in general moved in a very different direction.

29. On the contemporary development of theologies as reflecting a continuum of interests, see Hans Frei, *Types of Christian Theology,* ed. George Hunsinger and William C. Placher (New Haven, Conn.: Yale University Press, 1992). Friedrich Schleiermacher offered in 1830 the first such critical understanding of the different tasks of theology moving from retrieval to understanding and proclamation. See Friedrich Schleiermacher, *Brief Outline on the Study of Theology,* trans. Terrence N. Tice (Richmond, Va.: John Knox, 1970).

With little need to define themselves in the culture or over and against other forms of Christianity, the concern was primarily with the experience of God and how that was expressed and conveyed in the church's worship. Hence, Eastern Orthodox theologies have been primarily mystical and sacramental.

Anglican theologies are less easily characterized, in large part because no one strand of the tradition has assumed a clearly normative stature. Richard Hooker provides the first and classic apology for Anglicanism. Structuring his work around the question of authority and not around the Trinity as the means of giving a systematic expression to Christian belief, Hooker provides neither a systematic nor a dogmatic theology. Instead, he points back to the church. It is in and through the church that Christian faith is given, revealed and effected in Word and sacrament. It is then the ascetical and devotional theologies that may be thought characteristic of Anglicanism, especially as they are developed in a literary fashion, beginning with Jeremy Taylor, George Herbert, and John Donne. But, however appealing the poets may be, they too depend on the voices of other Anglicans who vary so greatly in their theologies. In the end, Anglican theology is not one thing. It can only be understood as varied responses addressing different challenges and questions in the community of faith.

This diversity at the heart of Anglican thought may prevent the reductionism of faith to some set of beliefs, as can too easily happen where systematic theologies or dogmatic theologies are at the center of a Christian tradition. The danger, however, is that the varied accounts are not easily connected. And what is true of theology in general is true of moral theology and ethics in particular.

As already indicated, at various times different questions have been asked and addressed regarding Christian faith and the moral life. A guide to holy living was the focus of Jeremy Taylor's two classics, *The Exercise of Holy Living* and *The Exercise of Holy Dying*. These texts were strictly speaking ascetical. They focused on the disciplines that form the Christian in holiness — prayer and worship, examination and devotional exercises, temperance in personal matters, and charity towards others. In addition, Taylor was a casuist. That is to say, he examined particular cases of conscience in order to provide guidance to individuals who might be confused about what to do. Always, the concern was in shaping the heart and mind so that what a person did would express and deepen the experience of the presence of God. Ethics was practical, uniting ascetics and casuistry.

The evangelical theology of John Wesley shapes ethics differently. Wesley was deeply influenced by the tradition of Jeremy Taylor, especially as developed by William Law in his *A Devout and Holy Life*.[30] This is reflected in Wesley's development of "holiness clubs" in his years of study at Oxford. These provided fellowship and accountability to the disciplines of faith — prayer, reading of scripture, preaching, personal witness, and acts of service, including visiting the sick and those in prison. For Wesley the exercise of holiness continued to be assumed as the way of life of a Christian. In this sense ascetics remains at the heart of ethics. Following his conversion at Aldersgate, Wesley's own work, however, focused theologically on Christian faith as a matter of conversion of the heart. Ethics as holy living required above all one thing: hearing and receiving "the saving Word" given in Jesus Christ. In this sense, ethics was understood and more narrowly shaped in terms of a theology of grace. Wesley's ethics is then given in his scriptural preaching, especially on Pauline texts.

In contrast to a focus on cases and disciplines or more theologically on scripture and the saving work of Christ, a whole other strand of ethics in Anglicanism has been philosophical. In no small measure English moral philosophy has sought to establish a common moral basis for society in terms of universal moral truths rather than in religious faith and piety, however much faith and piety were seen as true.[31] The task of ethics was to describe the basis of morality and its expression in terms of moral principles. The moral philosophies of John Locke, David Hume, and Joseph Butler, for example, were shaped by religious understandings but led to the development of

30. William Law, *A Serious Call to a Devout and Holy Life* and *The Spirit of Love,* Paul G. Stanwood, ed. (New York: Paulist, 1978).

31. On the history of English moral philosophy see J. B. Schneewind, *Sidgwick's Ethics and Victorian Moral Philosophy* (Oxford: Clarendon, 1977).

moral philosophy that increasingly narrowed to the logic of moral discourse separated from any theological foundation or focus.

In one sense, ethics as moral philosophy can be seen as the breakdown of an integrated account of the Christian life. The eighteenth century marks a decisive step in the radical break with a singular, Christian worldview. The new sciences — epitomized by Newton's laws of motion (for example, for every action there is an opposite and equal reaction) — understood the world in terms of cause and effect. No longer was the world conceived as expressing the mind of God, such that every action was understood theologically. The evangelical theology of John Wesley reflects this shift. Theology has less to do with what Richard Hooker spoke of as "laws" (which is to say, the divine purpose expressed in all of life) and more to do with the experience of God that causes faith (spoken of as grace or "justification by grace"). The truth of Christian faith was given in the effect on the believer caused by scripture. Scripture revealed the will of God towards us. In this change, the world of faith was narrowed to the world given in the Christian texts themselves. Evangelical theology was thus separated and even opposed to accounts of the world and human action informed by other sources. In this context, moral philosophy may be seen as a reaction to the narrowing of theological understandings by seeking a universal account of human behavior. Given the different sources, the scene is then set for increasingly separate and opposed accounts of Christian faith and morality, and for attempts to develop new unified understandings.

In reaction to narrowly evangelical or philosophical accounts of Christian faith and life, the Anglican Catholic revival began as "the Oxford Movement," so named because it was initiated by a series of *Tracts for the Times* written by Oxford dons — John Keble, Edward Pusey, and John Henry Newman.[32] They believed the church was lost between the anti-intellectual emotionalism of evangelicalism and a reasonable Christianity that spoke more of the present age than of a body of faithful people participating in the divine life centered in

32. John Henry Newman, et al., *Tracts for the Times* (New York: AMS Press, 1969).

prayer and worship. The development of Anglo-Catholic thought from its beginnings in the 1830s progressively sought a fuller, more unified account of Christian faith grounded in the life of the church.

The initial stage of development in Anglo-Catholicism was a historical retrieval of the beliefs and practices of the early church. At the heart of this retrieval was a sacramental renewal. As developed in liturgical renewal, the Eucharist was the central celebration of the Christian community. In Holy Eucharist the scriptural revelation in Jesus was enacted and present now. The larger vision of the renewal of the sacramental life of the church was inseparable from a renewal of the life of the church in the world. The church was the sacrament of Christ in the world. This vision of Christian faith and life was a medieval vision of a church that made sense of the world as it transformed the world in light of Christian faith.

As the early Anglican thinkers of the sixteenth and seventeenth centuries — especially Richard Hooker and the Caroline Divines, beginning with Jeremy Taylor — stood in this medieval world where the church was at the center of the village, Anglo-Catholics claimed themselves as the true heirs of Anglicanism. Given this vision, the task of Christian ethics was, as it was for Taylor, to provide guidance as a matter of practical piety. In the twentieth century, Kenneth Kirk gives the fullest expression to such an ethic as practical wisdom dealing with cases and ascetics, the disciplines that form and deepen the sense of the presence of God in our lives. At the same time, especially as the society is increasingly secularized and so no longer reflects a deep Christian ethos, ethics needs to offer a vision of society in light of Christian faith. Twentieth-century Anglo-Catholics increasingly turned to this task, most notably reflected in the thought of William Temple.[33]

While evangelical thought tended to identify faith with a particular understanding of the saving Word of scripture, Anglo-Catholics courted the danger of identifying the church with ancient rites and liturgical traditions — the very Catholic ways that were the original source of the Anglican/Protestant rejection of Rome. Fundamentalism among Anglo-Catholics was as great as that among evangelicals. As in

33. See above, notes 26 and 27.

every age, to prevent a fundamentalism, a unified understanding of Christian faith and life was needed which would draw together Christian faith as given in and through particular historical texts and practices and contemporary understandings of the world. The broad church or liberal church had sought such an understanding in deism in the eighteenth century, most significantly in the work of Joseph Butler. However, such a framework had finally led more to a philosophy of religion than a living, breathing faith of a people formed by the church. Still, some such framework was required in order to make sense of both evangelical and Anglo-Catholic claims.

Frederick Denison Maurice provided the most significant framework for developing an integrated account of Christian faith in which the conflicting claims within Anglicanism and more broadly in the Christian tradition-at-large could be drawn together.[34] For Maurice, scripture and worship were the revelation of the relationships that realize the value and meaning of life. Philosophical understandings that claim to be universal are gained only in the experience of particular historical relationships. Word and sacrament reveal by bringing persons into these relationships. Given this theological understanding, ethics includes the tasks of ascetics and casuistry, but these in turn rest on an understanding of the relationships that are good. Morality was a matter of honoring that which is of value by realizing the relations that are of value in the world. Theologically speaking, the task of Christian ethics is to describe life before God, or what Maurice calls "the kingdom of Christ."

As Maurice argues, a unified account of the Christian moral life requires above all a description of life in terms of the deepest sense of self, in terms of what a person most deeply loves and what will ultimately give meaning and wholeness to life. Such an account is Christian because it is grounded in Jesus Christ. This grounding is a matter of both knowledge and experience. Christians claim that they know

---

34. In contemporary theology Maurice's project is assumed and developed by H. Richard Niebuhr. See especially *Christ and Culture* (New York: Harper & Row, 1951), which concludes with F. D. Maurice (followed by a final chapter "A 'Concluding Unscientific Postscript'," added at the request of Niebuhr's editor).

what finally gives peace or wholeness to life because they have experienced it in their lives. They are Christian because this experience has been revealed in the story of Christ as that is known and experienced in the worship and ongoing life of the church. Christian ethics as a description of the Christian life depends, therefore, on a description of this life. As a matter of faith, the more particular focus of what has been called moral theology — the practical resolution of cases (casuistry) and the development of disciplines of prayer, study, examination, and service (the focus of ascetics) — only makes sense as a matter of living more deeply into this life.

In this introduction to the Christian life I want to offer such an account of the Christian life. This account is itself what Anglicans have understood as a practical piety. Christian faith is a way of life that is a matter of the deepening of the experience of God. To use a different metaphor, Christian faith is a life lived in the presence of God. Christian ethics is a description of that life. As a matter of practical piety, the Christian life is understood as sacramental, incarnate, and corporate. First, this life is revealed and effected by Jesus Christ as known through the church, specifically in scripture, worship, and the life of the Christian community. In this sense, Christ is the sacrament of God. Second, this life is incarnate. The presence of God is experienced in daily life. This presence is experienced as the power in the relationships that give meaning to life itself. Third, this life is corporate. Life in God connects us beyond ourselves. We transcend our individual, solitary worlds and are brought into a unity or community with all of being itself. In this sense we are drawn into a new covenant as we come to participate in the divine life.

[CHAPTER 3]

Incarnate Love

~

A N OLD ADAGE told to children and young adults is, "If you want to know what someone is like, ask, 'Who are their friends?'" How we relate to those near and similar to us and to those distant and different from us reveals who we are by showing the world in which we live. The first, those near, we call neighbors. The second, those distant and different, even when close at hand, we call strangers. The Christian life, like any other life, is revealed in these relationships to neighbor and stranger. This was clearly understood in the Hebraic-Christian tradition. These communities of faith continually and explicitly addressed the questions, "Who is my neighbor?" and "How am I to relate to him or her?"

These two questions pose the question of Christian faith from the bottom up. We began the first two chapters of this study by describing the central beliefs and features that Christians have had about Christian faith and life. We concluded that Christian faith is a moral life in which the love of neighbor is grounded in the worship of God. As such Christian faith has been understood by Anglicans as a matter of practical piety. To then understand this faith requires answering the questions, "Who is my neighbor?" and, "How am I to relate to him or her?" To see how the answers to these questions developed in Judaism and Christianity as religious questions is to understand how Christian faith grounds, enlarges, and deepens the moral life.

Two spheres of human life are central to how these two questions have been answered: the family and the understanding of human sexuality, and the stranger and what makes a person human. In this chapter I want to offer an understanding of the transformation of human sexuality and the understanding of the family effected by Judaism and Christianity. In the next chapter I want to describe the transformation of the relationship to strangers and specifically to the poor. In the broadest terms, this account will show that Christian faith is a matter of revealing and establishing those relationships in our lives that give meaning and wholeness to life. This means that for Christians the story of God, beginning in Judaism and culminating in the story of Jesus, reveals what is wrong and in error in the relationships that form human life and what is true and enduring.

The Transformation of Sexuality

Human sexuality has always been a privileged point in the human, religious drama.[1] Sex is a powerful religious threshold because it promises connectedness at the same time that it threatens our selves by drawing us into something other and different than we had known before. "Love" expresses the one side of sexuality. Sex promises that I will be related beyond myself, whether love is viewed as united in desire or as united in adoration and care. On the other side, we say, "I'm falling in love." Sexual attraction is beyond my power. It happens to me, over-

---

1. The understanding of sexuality developed here as shaped historically and culturally is especially informed by the works of Michel Foucault and Peter Brown. See Foucault, *A History of Sexuality. Vol. 1: An Introduction,* trans. Robert Hurley (New York: Vintage, 1980); and Peter Brown, *The Body and Society: Men, Women, and Sexual Renunciation in Early Christianity* (New York: Columbia University Press, 1988). An earlier version of this argument may be found in Timothy F. Sedgwick, "The Transformation of Sexuality," in *Our Selves, Our Souls and Bodies,* ed. Charles Hefling (Cambridge, Mass.: Cowley, 1996), pp. 27-42.

whelms me, threatens me. In French the word for sexual orgasm is *"une petite mort"* — a little death. In sexual relations there is always the loss of oneself in another. Sexual relations are the most intimate sphere of our lives, and thus pose the question of the bond or covenant that gives life.

In the ancient Near East in general and in the beginnings of the Hebrew people in particular, sexuality was experienced as part of the great rhythm of life.[2] As depicted in the story of creation account that opens the book of Genesis (Gen. 1:1–2:4a), all the world is created in complementary opposites, opposites that depend on each other and together yield life. Darkness and light, sky and water, water and land — together these produce the seasons and the conditions for seeds to grow and bear fruit. Fish, birds, and animals inhabit this world with the blessing "be fruitful and multiply" (Gen. 1:22). And so humans are an extension of this world. Created male and female, they are to "be fruitful and multiply, and fill the earth and subdue it" (Gen. 1:28).

This picture reflects a natural, organic world infused and permeated with desire. Human life is given in the participation in these cosmic processes. Sexuality ties persons to what they experience as a cosmic power, a power in which they lose themselves. In sexual relations persons transcend themselves and participate in the powers of creation, which were before and will continue after the death of each individual. Human sexuality, however, is more than a cosmic, vital force. Sexuality is also a language of mutual recognition. In this sense, sexual desire is focused in the desire to be loved and to love. In the mutual enjoyment and care of each other, sexuality is personalized.[3] What is desired is not simply the body but the life formed together, a desire for love and not only for the bearing and caring of children. The second creation story in Genesis (Gen. 2:4b-25), which follows the account of creation focusing on progeny, turns to focus on what may be called the covenant of love.

2. The biblical interpretations of Genesis 1–3 are nicely summarized in Lisa Sowle Cahill, *Between the Sexes* (Philadelphia: Fortress, 1985), pp. 45-56.

3. Paul Ricoeur offers such a description of the transformation of sexuality in "Wonder, Eroticism, and Enigma," *Cross Currents* 14 (1964): 134.

In the second account of creation (Gen. 2:4b–3:24), the story of Adam and Eve is told. Adam, the human one (*'adam*) is formed from the dust of the ground (*'adamah*). God then declares, "It is not good that Adam should be alone" (Gen. 2:18). So the human one is cast into a deep sleep. Woman is taken from Adam's rib. In this act man and woman are formed, only now distinguished as male and female (noted by the distinct words *'is* and *'issa*). Formed from one flesh, they are called to unity together. As the image of the rib taken from the side of Adam conveys, woman and man are made for each other. Spoken by man, "This at last is bone of my bones and flesh of my flesh" (Gen. 2:23). In light of this account of creation, the Christian tradition has understood sexual relations as a matter of companionship. Sex is personalized and becomes an expression of love. Sexual relations are a matter of mutual recognition and care for the other.

In contrast to this focus on love as the basis of our relationship between one another, the first account of creation (Gen. 1:1–2:4a) focuses on procreation. Humans are to "be fruitful and multiply, and fill the earth and subdue it" (Gen. 1:28). Sexual relations are placed in the larger purpose of progeny and the formation of a people.[4] The laws in Deuteronomy and Leviticus further tie together sexuality and procreation. As a nomadic and then as an agrarian people, children were essential to the economic viability and survival of the intergenerational household. The various codes of laws, therefore, restricted and regulated sexual relations in order to ensure the bearing and caring of children. Divorce was a right to be exercised when acts of sexual wrongdoing or impropriety threatened the household (Deut. 24:1). Similarly, incest and prostitution were wrong because they threatened the order of the household by undermining the family hierarchy.

---

4. For placing sexuality in the larger context of social history see Leo G. Perdue, Joseph Blenkinsopp, John J. Collins, and Carol Meyers, *Families in Ancient Israel* (Louisville, Ky.: Westminster/John Knox, 1997). For a review of work on the social and cultural understandings of sexuality and the moral and theological assessments of these understandings in the New Testament, see Lisa Sowle Cahill, *Sex, Gender and Christian Ethics* (Cambridge: Cambridge University Press, 1996), pp. 121-65.

The concern for procreation and progeny was heightened in the developing history of Israel, especially after the sixth-century exile in Babylonia. Upon the release of the exiled people, only some of the people returned to Judah; many had already been assimilated in Babylon. Within a few centuries Judah would be ruled by Greeks and later by Romans, and the people could no longer hope to become a powerful nation. In this sense Judaism is born in a period of anxiety over identity and survival. In this context, Judaism increased the emphasis on procreation, on bearing children, so much so that infertility itself became grounds for divorce. "Jewish teachers agreed that the purpose of marriage is to 'increase and multiply'; that one must accept whatever facilitates procreation, including divorce and polygamy; and that one must reject whatever hinders procreation — even a marriage itself, in the case of an infertile wife."[5]

Though progeny and love as companionship need not be opposed, the dominant tradition in Judaism came to subordinate companionship to procreation and progeny. With such a primary emphasis on children, sexual desire in marriage was consecrated in the larger context of bearing children. The forbidden might be desired — as in the case of David and Bathsheba — but such desire was increasingly never unadulterated and so without guilt. The goods of human sexuality thus came to be ordered hierarchically, beginning with procreation. Sexual relations as a matter of love and pleasure might be good but good only in the context of marriage, where they contributed to the formation of the family.

The personalization of human sexual desire in terms of both love and progeny is precarious, especially in the face of pestilence, famine, and warfare. Too easily the human person is lost from view. Instead, persons seek to secure their identity by a singular focus on their children or by seeking their own self-fulfillment in the embrace of the "beloved." Of these dangers, the greatest in Judaism appears to have been the idolatry of the family, of making the family the end of life itself. Women were subordinated to men for the sake of producing and rais-

5. Elaine Pagels, *Adam, Eve and the Serpent* (New York: Random House, 1988), p. 13.

ing children in order to ensure their survival. What was idolatrous was that the family — and by extension the nation itself — destroyed other goods central to the value and meaning of life. Such idolatry is appropriately called patriarchy.

Jesus reveals the larger, ultimate context of human life that redeems sexuality from idolatry. More, through his teaching, life, and death, he draws those who follow him into that context, into what may be called the deepest covenant of life. Or to use the dominant language of the gospels, Jesus proclaims and inaugurates the kingdom of God. In terms of human sexuality, this meant turning from a narrow focus on the importance of progeny back to mutuality — to a companionship not as given in kinship but as the embrace and care of the other as an end in him or herself. This revelation of the new covenant as a covenant of hospitality is given in Jesus' teaching on divorce and celibacy.

In the Gospel of Mark, Jesus responds to the question of whether it is lawful for a man to divorce his wife by quoting the Yahwist account of creation: "From the beginning of creation 'God made them male and female. . . . For this reason a man shall leave his father and mother and be joined to his wife, and the two shall become one flesh.' . . . Therefore what God has joined together, let no one separate" (Mark 10:6-9). In this and parallel sayings (Matt. 19:4-6), Jesus' call to love one another overthrows the most fundamental contract on which society is based: as man and woman, husband and wife, perform their respective parts, children will be born and bear the identity of the parents into the future. Instead, Jesus claims that men and women share in eternity now, in their love for one another. It finally makes no difference what the future brings. The unity of the person is given not in pleasure or procreation but in the embrace and care of the other.

Agape as a love that serves the other, embraces the other and cares for him or her, becomes a chief image of Jesus' call to discipleship. The other is to be loved without conditions. In such love grace is given; there is the kingdom of God. Marriage, therefore, is not a matter of doing something in order to achieve or realize something else. Instead, marriage is a matter of mutual commitment to love another, for better or for worse, regardless of consequences. The relationship is unconditional, without conditions, and hence a matter of steadfast love and fidelity marked by acceptance and trust. In marriage, this covenant of love is expressed in the commitment to abide with the other, to love until death. Love is not a matter of self-fulfillment or fulfillment through children; it is a love turned outward in the embrace and care for the other. This is exemplified in the change of relationship between parents and children as told in the Genesis story of Abraham's call by God to sacrifice Isaac (Gen. 22:1-19).

In ancient Israel, as in most of the peoples of the world, blood sacrifices were offered to gods as thanksgivings. Such sacrifices always carried with them overtones of seeking the pleasure of the gods. Still, sacrifice was first of all a matter of acknowledgment and thanks.[6] Now Abraham and his wife, Sarah, had not been able to have children. The promise that Abraham would be the father of a great and prosperous people had become folly. When Sarah miraculously became pregnant at age 90, Abraham's hope was rekindled (Gen. 15-17). When God then called upon Abraham to offer his first son, Isaac, as a sacrifice, all seemed lost. The faithfulness of Abraham was tested. That is to say, his trust was tested, whether God was the sole and sufficient source of life or whether meaning in life depended on children. So Abraham rose early in the morning, cut the wood for the burnt offering, packed it and other supplies on a donkey, and set out on a three-day journey to the place of sacrifice (Gen. 22). As the nineteenth-century philosopher Søren Kierkegaard developed this theme in *Fear and Trembling*,[7] Abraham must have been torn between his love of Isaac and his hope and trust in God. With fear and trembling he finally offers his son as a thanks offering; and in this offering a second miracle occurred. God accepts Abraham's offering and provides a ram to offer in place of Isaac.

The gift of faith is for Abraham knowledge of the true covenant with God. God does not ask or require food offerings or blood sacrifice but only the acknowledgment and thanksgiving for what is. In this

6. For a recent discussion of the meanings of sacrifice, see Gordon W. Lathrop, *Holy Things: A Liturgical Theology* (Minneapolis: Fortress, 1993), pp. 139-49.

7. Søren Kierkegaard, *Fear and Trembling and Sickness Unto Death*, trans. Walter Lowrie (Princeton, N.J.: Princeton University Press, 1954).

sense life is given in the offering of ourselves to God. With this offering comes a new relationship in which everything is changed. Like Abraham, husband and wife give up children as the basis of their hope in the future only to have children given back, but now not as their hope but as gifts from God. Children are not extensions of the self but persons with their own gifts and skills, their own distinctive sense of the world, their own humor and beauty. They call others to acknowledge them, to care for them, and in love to be drawn out with them into a future marked by such love. In other words, they call us into what I have called the covenant of hospitality.

In marriage as in life in general, the covenant of hospitality is what Christians call an eschatological reality. The reality may be realized here and now, but only in part and never fully. We live into this covenant. We come to know another person only over time. We are able to acknowledge another in his or her uniqueness, as different, ever more fully only as we abide with them over time. We come to support and care, delight and enjoy the other, only over time. Only over time do we discover that the mystery of the other person is far greater than we had imagined.

There is no straight-line progress in such matters of love. Where relationships deepen as covenants, they do so through the crises that form a life together. The danger is always that such a love will fail to enlarge, to draw us beyond our immediate concerns and goods. Instead, desire may narrow and come to rest on some extrinsic good such as children, success, self-sufficiency, or pleasure itself. Only as the household is connected to broader meanings and practices can the life of its members be shaped beyond itself.

The danger of idolatry is so great, however, that Jesus not only called for the reformation of marriage, he also at times called for the rejection of sexuality and marriage altogether.[8] In the Gospel of Matthew, Jesus says,

Not everyone can accept this teaching, but only those to whom it is given. For there are eunuchs who have been so from birth, and there

8. For the development of the argument below see Pagels, pp. 14-16.

are eunuchs who have been made eunuchs by others, and there are eunuchs who have made themselves eunuchs for the sake of the kingdom of heaven. Let anyone accept this who can. (Matt. 19:11-12)

As expressed in the Gospel of Luke, "Blessed are the barren, and the wombs that never bore, and the breasts that never nursed" (Luke 23:29). Jesus even goes so far as to identify celibacy with eternal life and marriage with death: "Those who belong to this age marry and are given in marriage, but those who are considered worthy of a place in that age and in the resurrection from the dead neither marry nor are given in marriage" (Luke 20:34-35).

Jesus' call to celibacy is among the most radical expressions of the gospel, to give up everything for the sake of the kingdom of God, to take up the cross in the renunciation of maintaining the world in order to be raised into God. What matters is the unreserved giving up of oneself in the care and embrace of the world about us. This response is the most radical response of faith in that everything is given up in order to enter fully into the covenant of hospitality. In this sense, the ascetic vows of celibacy, poverty, and obedience are not a denial of the world but a vow of hospitality, the giving up of oneself in the embrace of the other.

Asceticism offers a critical perspective on sexuality. Sexual desire for another arises in the body. It is strong and deep but also fleeting and ephemeral. Sexual desire is domesticated by tying it to a life together. The bonds of matrimony order sexual relations in the context of the household for the sake of forming a people (procreation, broadly speaking) and caring for another (companionship).[9] In this way sexu-

---

9. In ethics such understandings have been discussed in terms of the ends of sexuality. See Margaret Farley, "Sexual Ethics," *The Encyclopedia of Bioethics*, ed. Warren T. Reich (New York: Macmillan, 1995) 5:2363-75; Lisa Sowle Cahill, "Sexual Ethics," in *The Westminster Dictionary of Christian Ethics*, ed. James F. Childress and John Macquarrie (Philadelphia: Westminster, 1986), pp. 579-83; Helen Oppenheimer, "Marriage," *The Westminster Dictionary of Christian Ethics*, pp. 366-68.

ality is personalized, transformed from a natural power to a more enduring expression of human purposes. Sexuality remains a matter of physical pleasure that draws a person outside of him or herself. But physical pleasure is broadened and deepened as two people come to love each other and as that love is expressed in a life formed together and passed down to the next generation. At the heart of this love is the embrace of the other who is truly other. Such an embrace is a matter of being drawn out into the mystery of another person, a mystery full of surprise, evoking compassion and care, disrupting what was taken for granted even to the point of letting go of what had been the basis of identity. If, however, marriage connects a person only to a particular person or household and society, it cuts a person off from life. Instead of a covenant that is ultimately transcendent, such bonds are idolatrous, pretenders that place the human spirit in bondage.

In reaction to the idolatry of the household or fulfillment in love of another, this covenant has been imaged in terms of love as self-sacrifice. Such an understanding is a corrective to idolatry but is finally too narrow an understanding of this covenant. Certainly in the care for another, a person will sacrifice other possibilities. The embrace of another is a letting go in the sense of giving up the self for the other. But such sacrifice is only part of love. Love is first of all a matter of a welcoming embrace. In this sense, instead of sacrifice, love may be better understood as hospitality. The welcoming embrace, moreover, reflects a desire and pleasure to be in relationship. Love is in this sense a kind of desire and a kind of friendship.

Christians have taken three Greek words to describe what in English is denoted inadequately by the singular word "love": *agape* as self-sacrifice, *philia* as mutuality or friendship, and *eros* as desire and pleasure.[10] In the Christian transformation of human sexuality, these

10. On the history of understandings of love see Irving Singer, *The Nature of Love,* 3 vols. (Chicago: University of Chicago Press, 1984-87). On contemporary, Western theological understandings see Edward Vacek, *Love, Divine and Human* (Washington, D.C.: Georgetown University Press, 1994). In contrast to Western views, Eastern Orthodoxy understands love in terms of *eros* in light of God as understood in terms of energies and as divine *eros.* See Stanley Harakas,

three loves are not separate loves but integrally related. We embrace another because we desire the other. In this love we are drawn out of ourselves and into a relationship we find fulfilling. The good we enjoy is such that we seek to care and nurture the other, even to the point that we will sacrifice our own physical well-being.[11] The experience of God is given in these relationships. That is what is meant by saying God is incarnate, literally enfleshed in these relationships of love.

Idolatry and Moralism

This description of the transformation of human sexuality as a matter of love illumines from the bottom up the meaning of the basic Christian conviction that Christian faith is a moral life. This description more specifically illumines the Christian belief in one God and the dual claim that what *is* is good, and that sin is the consequence of a misplaced love, a violation of the first of the Ten Commandments: "You shall have no other gods before me." In other words, Christian faith is a way of life that turns away from idolatry.[12]

Idolatry arises as goods such as pleasure, the family, or our personal loves become the ends or purposes of our lives. As such they are gods. We live for them and cling to them because without them we cannot imagine living. Some particular good is honored, loved, and desired, so much so that it becomes the end of life. In this sense, idolatry is false worship, giving ourselves up to and binding ourselves to an object or person or cause that cannot ultimately connect us in the

---

Living the Faith: The Praxis *of Eastern Orthodox Ethics* (Minneapolis: Light and Life, 1992), pp. 54-56, 166-70. One contemporary Western theologian who sought to offer a philosophical account of the unity of these loves is Paul Tillich. See *Love, Power, and Justice* (New York: Oxford, 1954).

11. For such an understanding see Margaret A. Farley, *Personal Commitments* (San Francisco: Harper & Row, 1986), pp. 29-32.

12. A classic account of faith and idolatry is H. Richard Niebuhr, *Radical Monotheism and Western Culture* (New York: Harper & Row, 1958). A contemporary account of radical monotheism and the nature of idolatry is Edward Farley, *Good and Evil: Interpreting a Human Condition* (Philadelphia: Fortress, 1990).

sheer givenness of our lives. They are idols because they cannot sustain our trust, because they finally fail to have the power to connect us to that which is meaningful in the face of death.

Human sexuality is especially vulnerable to idolatry because it is an unformed desire. This is what Freud meant by saying that sexuality was polymorphic, that sexuality has many forms or shapes. Unformed in itself, sexual desire can become attached by association to seemingly endless objects. Desire for pleasure is often tied to the desire for recognition and affirmation. A man may find a woman sexually attractive because her recognition and desire would affirm him. Seeking affirmation of his own power, the relationship may only be attractive as long as he is dominant. Alternatively, a woman — to use the prevalent cultural roles — may seek to attract attention and recognition in a flirtatious manner, questioning, listening, and affirming the interests of a man. In this way she subordinates herself until she loses herself in a submissive role. She may then come to desire the dominant male and fear someone who is seeking a person in her own right. Specific styles of dress and self-presentation are often paired with these different attitudes of what are deemed masculine and feminine and thus themselves arouse desire. This almost infinite play of desire reflects the nature of idolatry. There is seldom a single idol that dominates misplaced love. Instead, idols are legion. All this evidences why Protestant Reformer John Calvin spoke of the human mind as a factory of idols.

Idolatry may be viewed as a form of addiction. Whatever the pleasure, from physical sensation to the pleasure of success to aesthetic delight, in idolatry desire is obsessive. The world is narrowed to the object of desire. The pleasure is sought above all and all the more because it is fleeting, temporary. Such pleasure is insatiable because it is unsustainable beyond the temporary moments of consumption or achievement. The social idols of family, tribe, nation, knowledge, culture, and religion are especially seductive. They offer a larger sense of connectedness because they extend beyond the individual and often beyond their lifetime. However, they are idols when they become the meaning of life instead of bearers of some larger meaning. They become idols when the connectedness of life depends on their continued existence. For example, the family is an idol when life born in the primary relationships in the family comes to be seen as possible only in the family as I know it. Similarly, a nation and a culture are idolatrous when they alone are seen as bearers of the larger purposes of life — from peace and prosperity to the cultural achievements of art and music. Religion too is idolatrous when knowledge of God is seen as possible only as given in a particular religion, whether that be my denomination or the Christian religion itself.

Where such idolatry reigns, all the forces available are used to extend and defend the social faith. Economic policy is measured first and last by whether it benefits the nation. Education teaches what supports the culture. Religion consecrates nation and culture. Political decisions are matters of power and interest. Military force is the last resort to extend and defend a way of life.

Where idolatry is highly developed, God is hidden and may remain so until the death of the idol. Family, tribe, nation, knowledge, culture, and religion all, eventually, come to an end. Some die of natural disaster, from the volcanic eruption of A.D. 79 that destroyed the ancient city of Pompeii to the famine and disease that continue to ravage the nations of the southern hemisphere. Others die of conquest, from aboriginal peoples to refugees of eastern Europe or central Africa, forced out of their lands by conquering tribes. And others die with the death of a nation or of an empire, from the sack of Rome to the tearing down of the Berlin Wall. Prophets, beginning with Amos in his prophetic oracles against Israel, have seen God in these deaths because in destruction and death what is finally true and enduring is revealed.

In religion, idolatry or false faith takes the particular forms of dogmatism and moralism. In the first, instead of a relationship, expressions of faith are reduced to right belief, to a particular expression of faith that reflects and supports a particular religious community. In the second form of idolatry, moralism, faith as a way of life is identified with a particular way of life expressed in specific rules for behavior. Dogmatism and idolatry can be liberal or conservative. For example, God may be reduced to a *paterfamilias* — to the father of the family whose power guarantees the blessing of the family as long as its members observe a set of moral commands that define who should do what and so the place and role of men, women, and children. The liberal response may be equally dogmatic and moralistic. Instead of ruler and provider, God is liberator and fulfiller. God calls people to be free from the dogmatism and moralism of their past. Autonomy and self-fulfillment are the ends of morality. For both, idolatry occurs as the faithful are identified only with those who belong to a particular community with its own more narrowly cultural understandings and prescriptions.

In ethics, the focus on particular moral principles and norms is always in danger of becoming moralistic. Moral norms are then the means by which to secure the idol. For example, human sexuality has been understood as directed towards two primary ends, the first called the procreative and the second called the unitive. These ends express the blessings of children and companionship. They are called formal norms, from the Greek meaning of the word "form." They express the shape or form of sexuality. This is in Greek thought understood as the *telos,* the purpose of sexuality, and in that sense the end of sexuality. They have also been called moral principles in the sense of being the basis for our actions. Whether called formal norms or moral principles, neither provides specific prescriptions or proscriptions. That is to say, neither tells what should or should not be done. These more particular judgments are called in Roman Catholic thought material norms. They indicate the material means, the way in which the ends and purposes may be realized. Protestants speak of these particular judgments as moral norms or rules.[13]

Several material norms or rules have been at the center of Christian sexual ethics. Given the end of procreation, openness to children has been one such specific moral norm. To be open to raising a family

13. For a current overview of discussion on norms and principles see James F. Childress, "Moral Norms in Practical Ethical Reflection," *Christian Ethics: Problems and Prospects,* ed. Lisa Sowle Cahill and James F. Childress (Cleveland: Pilgrim, 1996), pp. 196-217. On the Roman Catholic understanding of formal and material norms see Richard M. Gula, *Reason Informed by Faith: Foundations of Catholic Morality* (New York: Paulist, 1989), pp. 283-99.

is a good that challenges individuals to see and experience their sexual relations as connected to something larger than themselves. There may be good reasons for couples not to have children, but this does not mean that sex and children should not be connected positively in our hearts and minds. In turn, given the end of companionship, equality and consent are moral norms for sexual relations. Sexual union as a matter of love of the other person as a person means that they are not coerced into a relationship against their will. They must have the power to say yes or no and they must actually exercise that power if sexual relationships are to be unitive.

What is idolatrous is when norms become ends in themselves apart from the larger purposes and the goods of life. This has been done, for example, by prohibiting birth control. The prohibition against contraception makes sense only as the judgment is tied to the well-being of society. Prior to the modern advances in agriculture, transportation, sanitation, and medicine, human survival was continually threatened by famine and pestilence. Food production and distribution were precarious at best. Societies lacked any basic knowledge about infectious diseases and about effective means to prevent their spread. Given the absence of effective medical treatment, illnesses turned into epidemics that threatened the very existence of society. For example, the bubonic plague, what was called the Black Plague, swept through most of Europe in the fourteenth century and killed approximately one-third of the population. It is no wonder that in late antiquity at the time of Christ, each woman of childbearing age had to bear five children in order to maintain the population, especially since the average woman married by 14 and was dead by 23.[14] The demand to bear children was an imperative if society was to survive. The claim that sexual intercourse should always be open to procreation made sense.

Still, an absolute proscription against contraception is idolatrous. By expanding the human species without limits, the rest of nature is sacrificed, including entire ecosystems. The failure to limit family size also often results in the failure to support children, to care for them, to

14. See Brown, p. 6.

educate them, and to enable them to participate in society. Finally, the proscription against contraception fails to support sexual intercourse as an expression of love. Instead, the narrow focus on procreation has the consequences of denigrating if not outright rejecting sexual pleasure. Forbidden, pleasure in sexual arousal and the desire for pleasure accompanying sexual thoughts produce guilt and repression. A cycle easily begins. Guilt leads to hatred of the body, self-denial, further repression, increased guilt, rigorism, and rigidity in all matters dealing with sexuality.

Such is the consequence of the idolatry that moves from the good of procreation to a narrow focus on procreation and the moralism that follows. In reaction to this idolatry, the liberal response has sought to liberate sexuality from repression and rigidity. This, however, can lead to the opposite extreme, where self-fulfillment is the norm that determines everything else.[15] In reaction to a narrow procreative ethic, the relationship becomes everything. Idolatry is the danger. Care and enjoyment of the other devolves into mutual self-fulfillment. Each person is valued for the benefits and pleasures he or she gives. Instead of procreative norms, the norms are equality of power and mutuality. These norms alone become the norms for judging human sexual relations. The individual is the measure of all things. All that is of value is the individual pursuit of self-fulfillment.

The dynamics of idolatry arise out of the experience of change. Our experience of change is an experience of the fragility of what we love and the fragility of our own lives. Ultimately all things pass away. To love inordinately is to cling to something, to hold on, to seek to preserve and extend some thing or things beyond the ravages of time. We love inordinately because we love so much and cannot accept that what we love will perish. What we love is not idolatrous because it is evil. What we love is good. What is evil is our loving inordinately be-

15. For one collection reflecting contemporary discussions see Adrian Thatcher and Elizabeth Stuart, eds., *Christian Perspectives on Sexuality and Gender* (Grand Rapids: Eerdmans, 1996). For a critical appraisal of the Christian tradition in light of the tension between liberal and conservative concerns, see Cahill, *Sex, Gender and Christian Ethics*, pp. 166-216.

cause we cannot accept the good for what it is — finite, fragile, and always perishing. What is evil is attempting to make the particular goods of life into God, into what is absolute, enduring, and never changing.

Idolatry is inevitable. The self is formed in relationship to the particular goods of life. To speak of son and daughter, patriot, musician, athlete, naturalist, Epicurean, friend, and enemy is to describe a person in terms of his or her relationship to the goods of life. Our identity is given in ordering these goods or, more accurately, in our relationship to these goods. The possibility of defining ourselves too narrowly is always before us. We then fail to see beyond particular goods and trust too much in their power to give meaning to our lives.

The Covenant of Hospitality

Over time our relationship to what is good is defaced, diminished, or deepened — and sometimes both deepened and diminished. We have seen the divine life, but through a glass darkened by our idolatry.

In loss our idolatry is revealed. In this sense, loss is a matter of judgment that offers the possibility of new understanding and a new relationship to the goods of life. Christians have called this change conversion. Where this happens a positive revelation of a new way of life is given. The revelation of God is thus both negative and positive, a judgment and an epiphany. The first form of revelation is called *via negativa,* a negative way in that we know God in the death or negation of idolatry. The second form of revelation is called *via positiva,* a positive way, positive in that we have an epiphany or manifestation of God in our lives so that our relationship to God in life is deepened or altogether given anew. As idolatry reveals, these two ways are integrally related. The death of idols always reveals the religious question, "What ultimately has the power to sanctify life?" "What is ultimately meaningful in the passage of life?" This leads to the question of a positive revelation of God: "If idols are the corruption of our relationship to God, what is the right relationship?" "How is God present in the goods of our lives?"

As Christians have expressed these two ways, the *via negativa* and

[69]

the *via positiva,* God is judge and redeemer. For Christians, Jesus is this revelation of God. As described here in terms of human sexuality, Jesus judges idolatry in his condemnation of divorce and even marriage itself. In turn, Jesus offers another way. He lives out a new way of life and invites those who would hear to follow. As a positive revelation, Jesus reveals what has been variously referred to as the kingdom of God, a new covenant, Christian faith, incarnate love, or what I have simply called a covenant of hospitality. This positive revelation is then explored and developed by those who follow Jesus. They do so in different settings and in different ways as they seek to know and enter more deeply into this covenant of love. In the sphere of human sexuality Christians have followed two dominant ways, the way of marriage and the way of celibate religious communities.

Christian understanding and formation of marriage is a long process with a variety of accommodations to society — reflected, for example, in ownership and inheritance of property. Marriage, however, also offers a positive vision of the covenant of hospitality.[16] In marriage two persons vow to enter into this covenant. The vows themselves may be understood as threefold. First, the vow of marriage is to abide and care for the other, unconditionally, "for better for worse, for richer for poorer, in sickness and in health . . . until . . . parted by death." Second, in marriage, vows are made to be sexually monogamous, to forsake all others and to be faithful "as long as both shall live." Third, the vow is made to bear and raise children "when it is God's will."[17] Together, these vows express and effect what marriage

16. For the most comprehensive account of the historical development of marriage, including a review of historical studies, see John Witte Jr., *From Sacrament to Contract: Marriage, Religion, and Law in the Western Tradition* (Louisville, Ky.: Westminster John Knox, 1997). Witte develops this account in terms of (1) the Catholic sacramental model, (2) the Lutheran social model, (3) the Calvinist covenantal model, (4) the Anglican commonwealth model, and (5) the Enlightenment contractarian model. The models themselves reflect a critical response to the past and to new situations. The normative account offered here is closest to the Anglican commonwealth model as that was democratized.

17. *The Book of Common Prayer* (New York: Church Hymnal, 1979), pp. 427, 424, 423.

is. Life commitment, sexual exclusivity, and openness to raising children incarnate the love of God revealed in Christ.

Life commitment and monogamy are themselves vows of fidelity, to abide with the other in love. Each is an unconditional commitment to love another — for better or for worse, in living and in dying, forsaking all others as long as both shall live. In contrast, to commit oneself to abide with another as long as both shall prosper is a conditional embrace. Another is judged in terms of whether or not he or she will fulfill my needs, desires, and wishes. In such a relationship each person seeks to fulfill his or her perception of what the other wants, at least sufficiently so that his or her own needs, desires, and wishes might be fulfilled. When there is no mutual fulfillment, the relationship ends. Instead, life commitment expresses and effects an unconditional embrace of the other as other — in all of the other's distinctiveness, strengths and limitations, strivings and struggles, achievements and failings. Where there is such hospitality, honesty and vulnerability are possible, with oneself and with the other. Love itself becomes an embrace that draws each person out into compassion, care, and delight in the other.

Similarly, monogamy expresses and effects the love I have described as given in the covenant of hospitality. In marriage, sexual relations are placed in the larger context of forming a life together in love. Sexual exclusivity forms sexuality into an expression and realization of that love. Sexuality can be shaped in a variety of ways. At the extreme distance from intimacy, prostitution narrows sexual relationships to a physiological stimulus and response. Sexuality becomes narrowed to the point where another is experienced only as an object of desire. Sexual relations are then mechanical, a mere exchange of bodies. Experiencing their sexuality in this manner, persons become disconnected from their bodies. Their bodies are apparatus no longer connected to their souls, able to feel the desire for intimacy, express or invite vulnerability, embrace caringly, respond with the joy of spontaneity, or rest in and enjoy the presence of the other. Marriage seeks to shape sexuality differently. To commit oneself unconditionally, for one's life, to sexual relations with one other person alone is to consecrate sexuality so that it expresses and realizes love as a covenant of hospitality.

Openness to raising children, "when it is God's will," is the third feature or character of marriage as a covenant of hospitality. Acceptance and delight in the other as other is a love that extends outward — hence the primary images of embrace and hospitality. The Orthodox understand this in claiming that at the center of love is divine *eros*. Our deepest desire is participation in God, where God is best conceived as energy or power that overflows in drawing all of creation into relationship.[18] People become divine *(theosis)* in being drawn into a love which is forever going beyond itself in the love of the other. A love that stops with some one person or persons, tribe, or culture is idolatrous. Such love is the spark of the divine but is smothered if it is not given room to expand. Children are expressions of such love and, in turn, continue to call forth that love. It is in this sense that we speak of children as gifts from God. They are given to parents to love and care for. They are different, unique persons that must be cared for in their own right if they are to become themselves. In this sense, they are strangers who call parents out to love beyond themselves.

There may be good reasons not to have or adopt children. However, when the decision to have or not to have children is assumed to be a choice of parents, the danger is that children will be conceived as possessions instead of as gifts. Prior to reliable contraceptives it was impossible to assume that children were simply a matter of choice. They were then experienced as integrally tied to sexual intercourse, not as a matter of choice but as a matter of nature. Sexual intercourse was not experienced as a narrow affair between persons but as part of a love and desire that always extended beyond the individual, for better or for worse. Parents were ideally drawn in the embrace of one another into a larger embrace of children. Of course, the other side of unreliable contraceptives is that children could also be experienced as a matter of fate. Instead of gifts, another child could be an unbearable burden to a family struggling at its financial and emotional limits to feed and raise children they already had.

The larger point, however, is that openness to raising children is

18. Harakas, *Living the Faith*, pp. 54-56.

a concrete expression of the end of sexuality as a matter of the covenant of hospitality. To deepen their own participation in this covenant, couples need to be open to children. The decision not to have children, or to consent to the impossibility of having children, needs to be placed in this larger context, as a couple's positive choice made in the context of committing themselves to the covenant of hospitality. In summary, marriage is a positive expression of the covenant of hospitality. As such, the features of marriage are given in life vows to care and abide with one another, to forsake all others, and to be open to bearing and raising children in a life together.

Only in the life lived is the love given in the covenant of hospitality known. We are called into covenant — invited, welcomed, embraced; but as a relationship, the covenant of life is not something to be realized in some particular state. Our actual relationships are rather always *in via,* on the way, in the process of development, a matter of struggle, and thus both fragile and corruptible. Marriages offer a way to acknowledge and deepen the covenant of hospitality. However, marriages also fail, as evidenced by abuse, neglect, and, as the Orthodox say, by the death of the marriage relationship itself. It is for this reason that marriage is celebrated and initiated by a set of public vows.

Marriage vows express the commitment of two persons to form a life together. They are given because they express two people's deepest aspirations of who they are meant to be. They are, however, also given because two people are not yet there. Marriage vows are then public vows because a couple seeks and needs the support of the community. In turn, the community celebrates the marriage of two persons as a sign of what life together is meant to be. The vows thus express and bind the two together.[19] It is in this sense that marriage vows are sacramental: they signify and effect the covenant of hospitality.

This understanding of marriage is a *via positiva,* a positive way, of entering more deeply into the covenant of hospitality. This under-

19. See James M. Gustafson, *Ethics from a Theocentric Perspective,* vol. 2 (Chicago: University of Chicago Press, 1984), pp. 177-84. On the nature of vows, see Margaret Farley, *Personal Commitments* (San Francisco: Harper & Row, 1986), pp. 12-37.

standing is drawn from history. The historical reality is itself always circumscribed by particular social and cultural needs and understandings. But in this reality we experience the covenant of hospitality. In this sense, marriage is a normative vision of what may be called an eschatological reality. In other words, marriage as a covenant of hospitality is already but not yet, in part but not complete, experienced and seen but as if through a glass darkly.

As described in the beginning of this chapter, in ancient Israel the sphere of human sexuality was circumscribed most dominantly by progeny and purity. To be was to be a people, and that meant to have children formed in a distinctive identity. The meaning and experience of sexuality were inseparable from society. In contrast, in contemporary society sexuality is experienced largely as a domain of self-fulfillment, narrowly as pleasure and more broadly in a romantic relationship of intimacy that creates a nuclear family as a haven from a hostile world.[20] The meaning and experience of sexuality is individually personal. For women, this is in part a reaction to the way that sexual relations and roles have been patriarchal. By and large, marriage has served the interests of males, as reflected in divorce, property, and social roles that determine who decides and who does what work. The marriage vows that point to the covenant of hospitality are thus historically formed, understood, and circumscribed so that they consecrate a particular form of marriage. Still, the moral and religious claim is that marriage in the West has also been a *via positiva,* a positive way in which we are drawn more deeply into the covenant of hospitality.

The nature of this positive way is explored and tested as persons form together a range of domestic relationships. In an urban parish I participated in a series of discussions exploring how members of the congregation formed households and how they saw their households as households of God. These households included husbands and wives, husbands and wives with children, single parents, blended families (from divorce and remarriage), intergenerational households, ex-

20. Christopher Lasch, *Haven in a Heartless World* (New York: Basic Books, 1977).

tended families (including a single person or two as the extended members), gay and lesbian couples (with and without children), and celibate households of friends. Each household described its growth and struggles to form a life together.

These households are schools of hospitality.[21] As schools they educate and form their members in hospitality. The curricula may vary, but all contain certain elements. For example, a discussion of domestic ritual revealed the importance of meals together. Table manners and table talk are not profound discussions of things so much as profane interactions that reflect and effect dependence on each other, acceptance and care, and a sense of what matters. When then asked what was most important about the church for their lives in households, young and old and those between spoke of the church extending their lives, of opening them up and connecting them beyond themselves. In this way the church enabled marriages to form households as households of God.

Again, as this chapter has explored, the covenant of hospitality in marriage has been confused with other needs and interests that have been equally a part of marriage. In a word — which oversimplifies but makes the point clearly — marriage and the covenant of hospitality have been captive to patriarchal understandings of the purpose of marriage to secure identity against insecurity and anxiety by ordering and extending the family. Such understandings were embodied in the hierarchical relationships and roles in marriage between husband, wife, and children. The full nature of the covenant of hospitality is then seen only in light of critiques of marriage and by households that witness to alternative ways of forming domestic relations.

In the history of Christianity the most significant alternative household to marriage is the way of "religious," the way of men and women who have lived together in religious communities. As alternatives to marriage, these monastic households have formed their life together by rejecting sexuality in order to break with preserving the so-

21. On households as the basic context for faith see Tom Breidenthal, *Christian Households: The Sanctification of Nearness* (Cambridge, Mass.: Cowley, 1997).

cial order so that they might be more open and hospitable to God. They witness to the covenant of hospitality from a world apart from marriage and family. In this way they reveal more fully what is at the heart of the covenant that is ultimately redemptive. This brings us to the next chapter.

CHAPTER 4

Love and Justice

~

MY great-grandmother lived in a world of covenants, bonds that stretched out from her immediate family and extended family into the world of strangers. I recall my visits with her in a Baptist retirement home when she was in her 90s. She was still active, by then a resident for over 15 years and thus one of the elders. Though she had given up playing shuffleboard, she served as the librarian, sorting through donated books and sitting there as if on her porch, welcoming her neighbors to come and sit and stay awhile and explore what was new.

Perhaps it was those initial bonds of hospitality in her own life on the Minnesota frontier that formed my great-grandmother. Anyway, she knew that family was something larger than "kin" and greater than husband and children. The household was an opening to the larger world of strangers. Wherever she found herself she welcomed those about her and was thankful. She is for me an appropriate measure of the covenant which Christians have spoken about as hospitality.

Hospitality as welcoming the stranger is at the heart of an abiding love. As Moses says to the Israelites:

> The Lord your God is God of gods and Lord of lords, the great God, mighty and awesome, who is not partial and takes no bribe, who ex-

ecutes justice for the orphan and the widow, and who loves the strangers, providing them food and clothing. You shall also love the stranger, for you were strangers in the land of Egypt. (Deut. 10:17-19)

However, love as the covenant of hospitality is consistently misunderstood. Moses goes on to tell the Israelites to keep the commandments of God "so that you may live long in the land that the Lord swore to your ancestors to give them and to their descendants, a land flowing with milk and honey" (Deut. 11:9). In this way the Mosaic Covenant becomes a contract, an exchange, a "do this for that," instead of a relationship in which the embrace of hospitality is itself the embrace of God.

The revelation of the covenant with God as a covenant of hospitality has been a long process. The Hebrew people came to know the radical embrace of God's covenant from their own experience as wandering aliens. They knew God as strangers, as the alien poor in the foreign land of Egypt. With freedom in their exodus from slavery in Egypt and their return to settle in the land of Canaan, relationship with God was understood in terms of hospitality. To be sure, this covenant continued to be often seen as a privilege and a promise that they, in opposition to others, would materially prosper, if they would do justice and care for the stranger. But the deeper meaning of covenant and hospitality was recalled, particularly in times of crises where death had to be confronted. In confronting one's own death, the death of the society, and most poignantly the death of the poor and needy, the Hebrew people knew that God was not finally given in the particular goods of life, in wealth and prosperity, honor, progeny, or pleasure itself. As it was when they were the poor and alien, the only enduring covenant was in hospitality itself.

The story of Job explores this question of covenant: "What is the connectedness of life that gives meaning and wholeness in this world, where the righteous and innocent suffer and where finally all die?" The story of Job is set as a trial by God since God wants to know if anyone loves him for his own sake. Job is the righteous man; hence the evil and sufferings that befall Job are not deserved. The question is, does Job love God for God's own sake? The devil tests Job. His fortunes and health are taken away, his friends turn against him, and he is loathsome to his family. Job will lament, but he will not curse God. The trial ends with Job confronting God and God being revealed in the whirlwind, above the good and evil by which humans measure their life. God simply is. The covenant of life is simply given. All that humans can do is acknowledge God.

This sense of covenant as simply given was at the heart of the prophets' judgment against the Hebrew peoples. They variously proclaimed what God demands, clarifying the nature of the covenant. Amos is stark. God will be God, and all that matters is doing the will of God. In trampling down the poor into dust Israel so violated the covenant, the way of holiness, that the future is nothing but destruction. There is no escape. No longer can doing what is right be connected to human fulfillment. The day of destruction will not be revoked. All that can be done is justice.

The prophets Hosea, Isaiah, Jeremiah, and Ezekiel further develop an understanding of covenant as a relationship and not as a contract about the future. Hosea is the first to use the imagery of husband and wife. At the heart of the covenant of life is an abiding presence of love, like the love of a husband who takes back his adulterous wife. Israel has been a whore, but God will take her back. All that is desired and all that is important is entering into this relationship.

In different ways Isaiah and Jeremiah explore the character of this relationship that alone endures. For example, Isaiah develops the understanding that Israel's mission was to bear witness to God in the midst of its suffering, to be "a light to the nations" (49:6). As a suffering servant all may see that salvation is given in acknowledging the presence of God in all things, in the darkness as well as in the light, in the midst of chaos as well as the order of creation. Jeremiah, in turn, sees the covenant as a matter of the heart. The experience of God is such that what we do is not in order to win favor with God. Instead, what we do is an expression of our relationship with God (Jer. 31:33).

Still, while the prophets explore the nature of covenant in personal terms apart from securing their future prosperity, they fall back on the deep-seated conviction that — despite what has happened to the prophets themselves — to be in covenant will mean prosperity, if not in this life then in a life to come. Ezekiel holds the promise that "these bones shall rise again" (Ezek. 37). And Isaiah speaks in the most materialistic terms of "new heavens and a new earth" where Jerusalem will be restored as a city in which there will be no more weeping but only the sound of joy (Isa. 65).

The question of the nature of covenant is evidenced but not answered unambiguously by the prophets. The test case for understanding the covenant, though, remains human suffering. The innocent suffer, especially the poor, the sick, the hungry, and those who are strangers and aliens in a society. What then is the relationship with God that redeems life apart from future prosperity? Or in terms of Jesus' radical answer in the Beatitudes, "What is the covenant such that the poor are blessed?" (Luke 6:20)

As developed in the last chapter, the Hebraic-Christian tradition transformed human sexuality by shaping desire in terms of love. Such love was imaged as hospitality, as recognition, embrace, care, and enjoyment of the other. In turn, such love was contrasted with idolatry, in which the other became the means by which to secure the self, whether in pleasure, in the relationship itself, or in children. As suggested in this transformation of sexuality, life is given as a covenant of hospitality that not only transforms the most intimate relationships of our lives but establishes a new and different relationship with those who before were outsiders, strangers, aliens, and so especially with the poor and those in need. To better understand this love, we first need an understanding of poverty in late antiquity.

The Transformation of Poverty

The world of late antiquity, not unlike our global world now, was a world marked by a chasm between rich and poor. On the one side were citizens, those who had some property and so could participate in a social world that bore for them an identity through time. On the other side were the faceless ones of Roman law, those who had no standing in society because they had nothing. This was the world Peter Brown describes as "the drab, human wasteland of the poor." They were the silent majority who were, as a fourth-century astrologer said, "forever unknown, of low-born family, and doomed to a miserable life . . . always suffering and occupied in wretched tasks . . . their body and mouth . . . foul with horrible odor."[1]

A person could move quickly across this divide from having possessions to being entirely without provisions. Even for citizens with property, the threat of loss was ever present. In a moment all could be lost: poor weather and a failed crop, plague and illness in a village or city, or violent battle to gain or maintain control over land and people. The average life expectancy was less than 25 years. "Those who survived childhood remained at risk. Only four out of every hundred men, and fewer women, lived beyond the age of fifty. It was a population [in the words of John Chrysostom] 'grazed thin by death.' "[2] Even the landed aristocracy could not help but feel how precarious their lives were.

The sheer effort to sustain society, fueled by the anxiety of the real consequences of failure, could not help but reinforce the divide between those with and those without possessions. There was simply neither time nor profit in attending to the poor. The poor were thus faceless to those who had anything. Those who were acknowledged were part of an economy of exchange. Persons acknowledged those on whom they depended to provide and purchase goods or to protect and care for them and their families, as they would do in turn. Relationships were a clear hierarchy of mutual obligations. Each person did his or her part to preserve society as a whole.

The rich might give something to the poor, but such giving always reinforced roles and relationships. The rich gave to the poor as a sign of their standing, an emblem of their power and distance from those in need. As a Roman statue depicted, the rich stood over the poor and reached down to offer food. An embrace of the poor was unimag-

1. Peter Brown, "The Face of Poverty," The 1980 Hale Lectures, Seabury-Western Theological Seminary (unpublished), p. 7.
2. Peter Brown, *The Body and Society: Men, Women, and Sexual Renunciation in Early Christianity* (New York: Columbia University Press, 1988), p. 6.

inable. There was simply no sense of a common humanity. Christianity, however, changed all this. The relationship of rich and poor was transformed from mercy and benevolence to hospitality and compassion. In this was born the conviction of a common humanity, of a community of all people. This was, says Peter Brown, "the greatest single symptom of the end of the classical world in the Mediterranean."[3]

As in the transformation of human sexuality, the embrace of the poor as fellow human beings was a change in understanding and practice born progressively by the Hebraic-Christian tradition. In ancient Israel the stranger, the alien, the poor were not forgotten. This is reflected in the Holiness Code that was given to govern Israel as a new nation, no longer nomadic wanderers but a settled people of shepherds and farmers. A Sabbath year, the seventh year, was commanded. In that year the fields were to be left fallow and what then grew was to be left for slaves, laborers, livestock, and wild animals (Lev. 25:1-7). Similarly, the Deuteronomic Code required every third year that a tithe of the harvest be collected and given to the Levite, foreigner, orphan, and widow (Deut. 14:28, 29). And the Deuteronomic Code also included in the Sabbath year the demand that creditors be released from their pledge (Deut. 15:1, 2). The purpose of these laws was to insure that "there must be no poor among [the Hebrew people]" (Deut. 15:4). All persons were to have some means in order to participate in the society.

Here in these codes the demand for hospitality clearly acknowledges the stranger and those in need as persons, as fellow human beings. However, these codes reinforce the demand by connecting it to prosperity. Care of the stranger and all people in need was commanded as a requirement for this prosperity. Hospitality was the condition for fulfilling the covenant, so much so that covenant as hospitality was easily lost from view.

In line with the Hebrew prophets, Jesus calls those about him into covenant as hospitality itself. Jesus claims that those who follow him must love one another as he has loved them since there is no

3. Brown, "The Face of Poverty," p. 9.

greater love than to lay down one's life for another (John 15:12, 13). The covenant is fulfilled in the act itself. When this is known and acknowledged, there is a singleness of heart. Jesus' teaching and life, his death and resurrection, reveal and instill this singleness of heart. Parables such as the Good Samaritan (Luke 10:30-35) and the Prodigal Son (Luke 15:11-32) shock us by the complete, exuberant response to the stranger or person in need. There in the response is the kingdom of God.

The importance of the heart is so great that Jesus himself renounces all property — and with that power and privilege — and calls others to follow him into the kingdom by also becoming poor. This poverty he declares blessed. In poverty, as in his renunciation of sexuality and with that the obligation to provide for family and children, Jesus claims and Christians proclaim that God is fully present. Here is the abandonment of worldly power and the hope of securing the future.

This change in understanding of covenant may be understood as a change from an economy of exchange to an economy of sacrifice.[4] In an economy of exchange, relationships are a matter of "this for that." We are joined together as a matter of mutual benefit. This need not be narrowly individualistic, where cost-benefit is narrowly determined by a particular transaction, as between buyer and seller. A people may care for widows and orphans, but in an economy of exchange this is a matter of insurance. Care is extended to those in need in order that the same care will be extended to oneself or one's family. Whether short- or long-term, consequences are all important.

An economy of sacrifice is of another order. The self is given up in relationship with another. The meaning of this economy draws on the rich associations of the word "sacrifice." The meaning of this economy beyond cost and benefit is difficult to comprehend, at least in contemporary Western culture where nearly every relationship is measured in terms of an economy of exchange. The word "sacrifice" has come to narrowly mean giving up one's own claims. Sacrifice is thus associated with the diminishment and loss of the self. For example, in

4. Jacques Derrida, *The Gift of Death,* trans. David Wills (Chicago: University of Chicago Press, 1995), pp. 101-9.

a world of patriarchy men gain power and privilege at the expense of women. Women's roles, it is then said, sacrifice women for the benefit of men. Hence, any call for sacrifice should be rejected.

The broader meanings associated with sacrifice arise from the original Latin meaning of sacrifice, which was to make something sacred or to perform a sacred act.[5] Sacrifice had its origin in meals, in the offering of food to the gods. This could and did at times become a matter of exchange, of offering food to God or to the gods in order to gain favor and benefit. However, the sacrifice of food had a more fundamental character. The sacrifice acknowledged that human life is not self-created but is dependent on others and on the fecundity of the earth itself. We are not our own. Life and the conditions for our continued life are given to us. In making sacrifice humans acknowledge this fact with thanksgiving. The offering expresses thanks and praise for what had been received, whether the harvest of the fields, the blessing of a child, or the arriving at a new stage in life. Life is given in acknowledging and entering more deeply into these relationships that are the meaning and power of life, that draw persons out of themselves into that world.

For Christians, Jesus offers a perfect sacrifice. That is to say, he fully acknowledges and offers his life to God.[6] In this way he reveals and draws those who acknowledge him into relationship with God. In the language of covenant, of the relationship that gives life, Jesus reveals a new covenant. This covenant is not a matter of exchange but of hospitality. In response to this revelation, the church is formed, not as a set of beliefs or ritual practices but as communities of faith following a way of life that is celebrated in worship.[7]

5. See Leonel L. Mitchell, *The Meaning of Ritual* (New York: Paulist, 1977), pp. 17-21, 26-28.

6. The classical account of "the shape" of Jesus' life as then enacted in the Eucharist is Dom Gregory Dix, *The Shape of the Liturgy* (London: Dacre Press, 1945); for a contemporary account see Gordon W. Lathrop, *Holy Things: A Liturgical Theology* (Minneapolis: Augsburg Fortress, 1993).

7. This is the fundamental claim of sacramental theology beginning with Edward Schillebeeckx, *Christ: The Sacrament of the Encounter with God,* trans. Paul Barrett (New York: Sheed and Ward, 1963).

The early Christian disciples formed their lives in different ways.[8] Some persons became solitary ascetics, most notably the desert fathers like Anthony, who tore himself altogether from the fabric of society. Others, such as the monastic brotherhoods formed by Basil the Great, gave up their private possessions in order to share together in an alternative Christian society. From the earliest beginnings of Paul, still others formed communities in the cities and villages where they lived and worked. Each of these individuals and communities explored the meaning of the gospel in the way in which they lived out their lives.

The most radical exploration of the meaning of poverty in terms of the gospel was undertaken by the ascetics as they took literally Jesus' command to the rich ruler to sell all that he had and to come and follow (Luke 18:22). In addition to giving up their possessions, the ascetics — whether solitary or living in community — adopted a range of body-denying disciplines, from living on gruel to staying up all night in prayer in order to be ready for the return of Christ.[9] Such actions connected with voluntary poverty were not simply a matter of rejecting the body. More centrally, they were means of disciplining the passions, of killing desire and rejecting the roles and relations of society in order that a person would be naked before God. These explorations of "lady poverty" hold the promise of illumining how the ascetics came to experience God in hospitality, in the singular embrace of the poor beyond any economy of exchange.

To state the conclusion in answer to the question, in assuming actual poverty in imitation of Christ, ascetics identified with the poor and found that poverty was not the absence of God but a new openness to God. In poverty they discovered a grace and reconciliation they had not known before, a reconciliation with God and with the whole world. All

8. See, for example, Brown, *Body and Society,* and Wayne A. Meeks, *The Origins of Christian Morality: The First Two Centuries* (New Haven, Conn.: Yale University Press, 1993).

9. On the contemporary discussion of asceticism see *Asceticism,* eds. Vincent L. Wimbush and Richard Valantasis (New York: Oxford University Press, 1995).

the world was God's. Society was not a matter of a commonwealth to be achieved in history. All people were already the people of God. From outside Christian faith, the irony is that the ascetics who rejected society created a new society. Paradoxically, and more accurately, in poverty the ascetics were brought into the community which alone endures. Two examples illustrate this transformation: the Pachomian community in the walled cities of the Middle Nile in Egypt, and the formation of brotherhood communities and of hospitals for lepers by Basil the Great in Cappadocia across the Mediterranean.[10]

At the lower end of the Nile River in Egypt the land was rich from annual flooding and so afforded a prosperous civilization. The great city of Alexandria was itself at the mouth of the Nile. As the flood plain decreased going up the Nile, poverty increased. Here "the heaviest population in the ancient world squatted in a poverty that had been quite legendary since Hellenistic times." Walled villages sought to protect those who worked the land available for crops from nomadic robbers. As a Christian growing up in these conditions, Pachomius turned "the blank hopelessness of the rural poor into its only possible alternative: a life made tolerable, dignified, even lovable by being lived out in terms of the new Christian symbolism of the poor."[11]

What Pachomius did, simply put, was transform the walled village from a battleground to a place "under Mercy." Instead of "pitting kin group against kin group in bitter competition for limited goods," the village was organized around households of about ten males each, open to and often recruiting directly from pagan families. The poor were embraced and made members of a community. Celibate, these communities had no end other than sharing a common life lived in prayer and hospitality. They would even boast that "some of them died without having known money." "What is a greater vision," asked Pachomius, "than to see the invisible God in the visible man? We, the little men . . . must be compassionate and merciful to each other."[12]

10. These two examples were offered by Peter Brown in his 1980 Hale Lectures, "The Face of Poverty" and "Towards a Sociable Philosophy."

11. Brown, "The Face of Poverty," p. 27.

12. Brown, "The Face of Poverty," pp. 28-30.

In Cappadocia the situation was quite different from that of the Middle Nile. The population was spread more thinly in the high plateau between the Mediterranean and the Black Sea. The economy was based on sheep and horses, many of which were raised to be sold to those further west towards Rome. Here by the fourth century "a strong and benevolent form of traditional Christianity" had arisen "controlled by a few great families."[13] Still, the world for most people was comparatively stark. Frequent drought left thousands dead of hunger and forced others into debt and poverty. The few opportunities to be found were within the political system of ecclesiastical patronage.

Basil's own aristocratic upbringing had prepared him for a high-ranking position in his ecclesiastical social world. However, Basil believed that in this world of church and society "Christian love had become circumscribed, city by city."[14] A different way was required in order to be faithful to Christ. He took quite literally Christ's call to poverty and to give to those in need. This led Basil to establish celibate households or what he called "brotherhoods." These communities gave up personal property in order to live a common life of prayer and hospitality. They raised their own food. What surplus they had they didn't keep as a hedge against the future for when a crop might fail. Instead, they went out from the community to give whatever surplus they had to the poor.

These celibate brotherhoods were for Basil but one means of realizing Christian faith. Basil also embraced lepers by establishing monastic communities to provide for their care. Disfigured, lepers were in the ancient world outsiders, cast outside because of their illness, which most believed was punishment for their sinfulness. Later called *Basileias* in honor of Basil, these communities are the forebears of hospitals, literally places of hospitality where the sick who were rejected by society were welcomed.

Both brotherhoods and *Basileias* were not narrowly separate societies so much as specific Christian communities that served the larger church and world by bearing witness to what all were to be. Above all,

13. Brown, "Towards a Sociable Philosophy," p. 3.
14. Brown, "Towards a Sociable Philosophy," p. 5.

for Basil, "to be poor and not merely to be a philosopher 'above wealth' was both the most sure mark and the most searching discipline of the true Christian."[15] Hospitality, in this sense, reflects a fundamental change of identity and hence attitude. This is not love understood as the fulfillment of the self in the love of a particular other person, as when lovers fall in love with each other. Instead, this is a love that draws the human person outside of him or herself into the embrace and care for another who is truly "other."

Benedictine communities established some two hundred years later similarly stood apart from the attempt to establish human identity in history through children and wealth, progeny and property. Drawing on Basil's own *Shorter* and *Longer Rule,* Benedictine communities assumed celibacy and poverty in order to follow a rule of life with its three-part discipline of prayer and worship, reading and study, and work.[16] Benedictine communities were communities of poverty in the sense that the community abandoned itself before God. While these communities were not as active in the direct service to the poor, again strangers were welcomed, not as a matter of benevolence, of reaching down to the poor, but as a matter of identification. The poor were embraced because, as reflected in the story of Lazarus and the Rich Man (Luke 16:19-31), there is no divide between rich and poor. However, as Benedictine communities developed, the practices of the community often secured the provisions of life and even prosperity until the religious were poor, naked before God, in name only. In turn, instead of embracing poor strangers, they may have stopped them at the gate.

Again, voluntary poverty does not ensure but offers the understanding that love is not a matter of the survival and prosperity of the individual or community. Instead, love is a matter of being drawn out from ourselves in caring for those beyond us. The deepest and most enduring connectedness of our lives is not in some reunion of the separate, as when lost lovers are united in love. We are not fulfilled or rec-

15. Brown, "Towards a Sociable Philosophy," p. 17.

16. Saint Benedict, *The Rule of St. Benedict,* ed. John Chamberlin (Toronto: Pontifical Institute of Medieval Studies, 1982).

onciled in being completed but in being emptied of ourselves and drawn beyond ourselves. Love is the joy given in the other, the desire that they be, and the care for them in their being.[17] Such love is given in all of our relationships — lover and beloved, parent and child, friend with friend. But love is known in its essence, at its heart for what it is, in the embrace of the poor and stranger. Here there is no confusion of fulfilling my need in the love of the other. There is no sense that I love because of what the other can do for me. In those in need we are simply called to acknowledge the worth and value of the other, we are invited to love and care in a way that draws us out of ourselves in union with all of creation.

In summary, the fullness of our lives is given in the covenant of hospitality. Reconciliation is given as this covenant is acknowledged and lived in all of the relationships of our lives, from the most intimate relationships with family and friends to the relationships we establish with the outsider, with the stranger. This is where God is present in our lives. Faith is in this sense a way of life, the order of things, as that which connects us to what is finally and ultimately worthwhile.

The Nature of Justice

While we may say that God calls us in the embrace of the stranger, it is not clear what that means for ordering and directing our lives. Poor and naked before God, the religious ascetics may know both that they meet God in the embrace of the poor and that they share a common humanity with all people. But it is not clear what they should do with the resources that have been given them. Should they, for example, like Pachomius form a walled city "under Mercy," or, like Basil, should they establish a hospital to serve those in need? Once a community is established, should they care for those who are sick or dying among themselves or should they "let the dead bury the dead" (Luke 9:60) so that they can serve the stranger at the gate? Whether it is the cloak the

17. Margaret A. Farley, *Personal Commitments* (San Francisco: Harper & Row, 1986), pp. 29-32; see ch. 3, note 10.

monk wears or the hours he spends each day, how to share or distribute limited goods is the question of justice. The shape of the Christian life as a covenant of hospitality is the source of our common sense of humanity. As such it calls for justice to all but does not itself answer such questions. These questions are rather a narrower focus of the discipline of ethics.[18]

Justice itself simply means fairness, to give to another what is his or her due, what another deserves, because equals should be treated equally. In Hebrew thought, justice and righteousness mean the same thing: to be in right relationship. These definitions of justice, however, are formal in the sense that "do justice" does not indicate what is the basis of equality and hence what is another's due or what is the character of right relationship.[19] The content of justice comes from specific claims, for example, "all men are equal" or "all people are equal"; therefore, all persons should be given those basic goods necessary to being human, to physical survival and to participation in society. Roman Catholics claim that this is the most basic claim of justice. Persons must not only be fed and sheltered and cared for in sickness, but persons must have other goods and opportunities, such as education, in order to work and more broadly participate in society.[20]

The difficulty in making decisions about our lives is not in the abstract but in the concrete. What, after all, are the basic needs or requirements for persons to be members of the society? While people

18. The argument here that justice is an account of what should be done in order to live out hospitality follows those who would argue that universal moral principles arise from and give expression to central features of specific historical communities. In this sense, universalists and communitarians need not be opposed but may be seen as offering different accounts of the moral life arising from their different concerns. See Michael Walzer, *Thick and Thin: Moral Argument at Home and Abroad* (Notre Dame: University of Notre Dame Press, 1994).

19. On the nature of justice see the National Conference of Catholic Bishops (NCCB), *Economic Justice for All: Pastoral Letter on Catholic Social Teaching and the U.S. Economy* (Washington, D.C.: NCCB, 1986), paras. 28-84.

20. *Economic Justice for All,* paras. 77-80. On membership as essential to justice see Michael Walzer, *Spheres of Justice: A Defense of Pluralism and Equality* (New York: Basic Books, 1983), pp. 31-63.

may agree about what is needed for physical survival, they disagree about what opportunities and levels of goods and services are necessary to participate in society.[21] For example, what level of education needs to be available in order to participate in society and not be forever doomed to a role of dependence linked to minimum wage and unemployment? Or, what resources must be provided to insure transportation that makes it possible to pursue education or gain employment?

The most comprehensive contemporary attempt to specify such basic human needs has been the development of "The Universal Declaration of Human Rights."[22] Civil and political rights indicate what is necessary to honor the intrinsic worth of the individual: to guarantee freedom of thought and expression, freedom from arbitrary arrest and torture, freedom of movement and assembly. Economic, social, and cultural rights indicate what goods must be distributed to all in order to insure their participation in society. These include the right to education, the right to health, the right to work and a fair wage, and the right to the protection of the family and a people's cultural history.

Still, even where there is some agreement on levels of basic justice, the problem remains what to do when not everything can be done. Apart from basic justice is what is called the question of distributive justice.[23] When there are fewer jobs than job seekers, it is impossible to distribute the jobs equally to all people. When there are limited medical resources and significantly different medical needs, not all needs can be met. Even more, it is impossible to make provision for each of the different spheres of justice. Funds for public health, medical treatment, education, disaster relief, police and fire protection, and

21. See Walzer, *Spheres of Justice,* pp. 64-83.

22. See John Kelsay and Sumner B. Twiss, eds., *Religion and Human Rights* (New York: The Project on Religion and Human Rights, 1994); see also NCCB, *Economic Justice for All,* paras. 79-82.

23. For the development of the nature of justice in terms of both basic justice and distributive justice see Walzer, *Spheres of Justice,* and the now contemporary classic of John Rawls, *A Theory of Justice* (Cambridge, Mass.: Harvard University Press, 1971).

new economic investment may all be argued as essential in order to insure basic justice. However, when all cannot be done, decisions must be made not only within each such sphere but between them as well.

In order to decide who should get what, several different kinds of reasons will be given. Most often cited are need, benefit, merit, contribution, and effort.[24] Concern for basic justice often focuses first on need. If you can't feed all, feed the neediest. If you can't provide shelter for all, shelter those most in danger from cold and heat. Need, however, is seldom adequate in itself for deciding how to distribute limited goods. Some people, therefore, say that those most likely to survive in a time of famine should be fed and sheltered first. Their short-term care offers the greatest long-term benefit. Here the argument is that in matters of distribution, need should be balanced by benefit. Decisions should be made in light of what will benefit the most people.

Closely related to benefit is a concern for contribution. Should not food and shelter be given not only in terms of what will most benefit people but in terms of who will be able to make the most contribution back to society? Should not parents be fed and sheltered first because they can then better care for their children? Should not training and education be developed and offered to those who can contribute the most back to society?

As these examples suggest, goods and opportunities are distributed by making some judgments about need, benefit, and contribution. These judgments are judgments about the consequences in distributing goods and opportunities. A final decision of what to do, though, must also be weighed against judgments about the person, about the extent to which they deserve preference because of their capacities, skills and talents, or sheer effort. For example, many would say that a position of leadership — perhaps a director of some imagi-

24. For the development of the criteria of distributive justice and, by example, their application to the question of access to health care, see Gene Outka, "Social Justice and Equal Access to Health Care," *The Journal of Religious Ethics* 2 (Spring 1974): 11-32. For a philosophical account of distributive justice see Nicholas Rescher, *Distributive Justice* (Indianapolis: Bobbs-Merrill, 1966).

nary cooperative providing food and shelter — should be offered to someone who has the skills and desire to do the job. This person, we say, merits the job. Of course, a person might be offered a position of leadership also on the basis of the contribution they may be able to make apart from merit. The younger person or the older person, the man or the woman might be hired for a position, other things being equal, because of the contribution they could make as a role model for others.

Distributing goods and opportunities is complex, both because persons receiving goods and opportunities are different in need, ability, and interest, and also because the goods themselves are different in kind. For example, the goods necessary for survival and participation in society are different in kind from what tastes good to an individual. Basic justice claims that all persons should have the goods necessary to survival. Entertainment, though, is a matter of preference, best left to the effort of individuals. So, for example, the choice of seats to a baseball game is arguably best left to those who are first in line.

Given differences in goods and persons, several reasons will often be given for distributing goods and opportunities. Jobs should generally be given on the basis of merit and contribution, along with effort which is often viewed as itself a matter of merit. Primary and secondary education should be offered to everyone on the basis of individual need and society's benefit. At the same time, specialized opportunities should be offered on the basis of merit and contribution. Effort again may be important when all else is nearly equal. The ongoing public debate over affirmative action or quotas, actually setting aside a certain number of jobs or openings, is an argument about justice, about what is fair for the individual and for society in both the short and long term.

Questions of justice are the most complex questions in ethics because of the different questions that must be answered. Basic justice raises the question, "What are the goods of life?" The second question is, "How do we distribute these goods?" This is the question of distributive justice. And to these two questions is added a third, "Who is to decide what to do?" This question is called procedural justice. For example, a majority vote may be an appropriate means of decision-making for a group determining some matters about their common life, perhaps whether or not to paint the interior of their meeting room. In medical treatment, however, it is generally agreed that in order to honor the value of the individual, patients should be the authors of their lives; they should decide what treatment they should receive. Still, the question remains, what procedures should be used to decide if patients don't understand what is happening and so are unable to make "informed" decisions? If they cannot make a decision — for example, because they are too young or too old to comprehend what is happening — who should decide? Again, the questions of justice are the most complex questions of ethics because they involve the whole of ethics: What is good? What should be done? Who should decide?

In the complexity of defining basic justice, determining the basis for distributive justice, and developing the processes for procedural justice, what is often lost from view is the religious ground of justice. The call for justice focuses on the assertion of claims of justice and human rights against claims of possibilities and priorities. The desire for justice, however, is given in the experience of the covenant of hospitality. Only in the covenant of hospitality do we acknowledge that we share a common humanity. In this is the ground of justice.

Law and Gospel

The relationship of justice to Christian faith as given in the covenant of hospitality has been understood in terms of love and justice.[25] Beginning in ancient Israel with the Ten Commandments, the summary of the law is understood in terms of love. Drawing together the summaries in Hebrew scripture (Deut. 6:4; Lev. 19:18), Jesus answers in the Gospel of Matthew the question, "Which commandment in the law is the greatest?" He says, " 'You shall love the Lord your God with all your heart, and with all your soul, and with all your mind.' This is the greatest and first commandment. And a second is like it: 'You shall

---

25. See Gene Outka, *Agape: An Ethical Analysis* (New Haven, Conn.: Yale University Press, 1972), pp. 75-92, 291-312.

love your neighbor as yourself.' On these two commandments hang all the law and the prophets" (Matt. 22:36-40; see also Mark 12:28-31 and Luke 10:25-28).

Justice is then understood as the consequence and expression of love. This life of faith is summarized by Micah as "do justice, love kindness, and walk humbly with your God" (Mic. 6:8). Given the love of God and neighbor, a person is just and acts justly. Here love is first of all a verb, a matter of the heart that expresses a person's deepest desire and intention. We say, "I love," but we don't normally say "I do love." Justice, on the other hand, is a noun or adjective, a matter of action or a matter of character describing the person who acts justly. So we say, "do justice" or "she is just." Together, love and justice inform each other.

Our hearts and minds determine what we do. A loving person acts justly. What we do, in turn, shapes who we are and what we desire and will. To do justice is to treat others fairly. In this response to another, love may be born. At the least, without justice there is no love. In this sense justice is the form or shape of love. Similarly, while hospitality is the ground of justice, justice is the response of hospitality. It is then inadequate to claim that hospitality requires only the interpersonal embrace between persons. Instead, law as the form in which justice is claimed is integral to hospitality.

To use the image of Emmanuel Levinas, the human face calls us to acknowledgment and response. Here in the face is the source of obligation.[26] But never do we see and respond to the pure face, to the call of recognition beyond understandings of the other, understandings that are shaped socially and culturally. The face is always something of an icon. Through the features of the face a person is present as an individual person having a will of his or her own that demands recognition. At the same time, the features of the face are a mask that we inter-

---

26. Emmanuel Levinas, *Totality and Infinity: An Essay on Exteriority,* trans. Alphonso Lingis (Pittsburgh: Duquesne University Press, 1969), esp. pp. 187-247. See also Thomas W. Ogletree, *Hospitality to the Stranger* (Philadelphia: Fortress, 1985), pp. 35-63; and Edward Farley, *Good and Evil: Interpreting a Human Condition* (Minneapolis: Fortress, 1990), pp. 31-46.

pret and to which we respond. We hear the distinctive call of another in a particular face that is always interpreted. Taken-for-granted interpretations and expectations of others are always present in the encounter between two persons, even as the encounter is a meeting of persons in the present.[27]

For example, I meet a woman in grief at the sudden death of a parent or child. She may sob or simply stand mute. I recognize her from within a frame of interpretation. She then looks at me. Our looks embrace. We touch each other. We are not then simply actors playing scripted roles. We encounter each other. Our interpretative frameworks abstract typical aspects or elements that connect our experience as common. In the encounter, though, I meet another who is unique. Her experience is unique and cannot simply or narrowly fit into my interpretative framework. My response is not a recipe, not the kind of response we call wooden. Instead, I hear and respond to *this* woman. My interpretative lenses are thereby variously refined or broken and transformed in light of this encounter. They, however, never cease to be a part of my understanding and response. There is, in this sense, no pure encounter.

Law as the form of justice is then necessary for a growing recognition of the other beyond conventional and culturally conditioned expectations. The demands of the law break open the icon that defines as well as presents a person. In this way the law calls us to acknowledge and respond beyond the features by which another has already been defined. For example, laws demanding equality of opportunity break open expectations of a woman's place. Laws condemning the use of

27. Drawing on the phenomenological analysis of Edmund Husserl and the analysis of human action as social by Max Weber, Alfred Schutz offers the most thorough philosophical analysis of the nature of interpretation in interpersonal relations. See Alfred Schutz, *Collected Papers II. Studies in Social Theory*, ed. Arvid Brodersen (The Hague: Martinus Nijhoff, 1964). In Christian ethics the play between interpretation and the interpersonal encounter stands at the center of the work of H. Richard Niebuhr, especially *The Responsible Self* (Harper & Row, 1963). For a more philosophically refined account developing Schutz's analysis in terms of moral decision-making, see Howard L. Harrod, *The Human Center: Moral Agency in the Social World* (Philadelphia: Fortress, 1981).

land mines as a means of military defense demand acknowledgment of people otherwise forgotten because they were implicitly defined as subordinate to the ends of politics.

In this way the law indicts wrongdoing and questions the heart of the individual. This has in the Christian tradition been called the juridical function of the law. The law is like a judge. But, as the tradition also knows, the law is more than a judge. The law is also a teacher, in what is called the pedagogical function of the law.[28] Judgment rests on some sense of a standard or some such positive claim. This moral sense of the law arises only because the law resonates with a deeper sense of what is true about our lives. The argument in this account of the Christian life is that the law is given as moral because it resonates with the call for recognition given in the face of the other.

The power to enforce the law, in turn, changes behavior and thereby the encounter between people. As women assume jobs traditionally held by men, women are seen differently. Their distinctive needs, interests, and concerns are given voice as they literally embody these jobs in new ways. New opportunities are, therefore, given for recognition and response. In short, the covenant of hospitality is deepened in the relationships that form our lives. In turn, the law banning land mines extends our recognition to those we too easily forget. Law gives opportunity for broadening the covenant of hospitality. In both ways, the law gives voice to the other, without which the world is narrowly contracted and consecrated in terms of roles and expectations. The law — or more accurately justice as the realization of the demands of law — does not itself realize the covenant of hospitality. But the law is necessary in breaking open expectations and embodying new relationships that together make possible both the deepening and the broadening of our participation in the covenant of hospitality.

The experience of law is called conscience. In this sense, conscience is imaged as the voice that speaks to us, condemns and ques-

---

28. In addition to the juridical and pedagogical functions of the law, there is the civil use of the law, what I will allude to in the next paragraph as "the power to enforce the law." See James M. Gustafson, *Protestant and Roman Catholic Ethics* (Chicago: University of Chicago Press, 1978), pp. 12-20.

tions us, because it senses what we should do and be. And like law, conscience has a dual reference.[29] On the one hand, conscience is a social conscience. The voice we hear is the voice of society embodied in the written and unwritten laws of society. On the other hand, the voice we hear is the voice that speaks individually and that we experience as an absolute demand. This is the voice we have heard in the face of the other calling us to acknowledge and welcome him or her. This is the voice of the stranger who calls us out of ourselves into a new world where strangers are friends.

As justice is a step removed from love, law also is at least one step removed from the interpersonal encounter. Its moral power comes from the interpersonal call or demand of another for recognition as a fellow human being. The law itself abstracts from this interpersonal encounter in order to specify what ought to be done. The law is like a recipe. Law is universal, at least in the sense that all persons in such and such circumstances should act in a certain way. This is what makes law *the law*.[30] However, as a particular recipe, law always reflects social and cultural understandings that reinforce the ways things are. As the cultural anthropologist Clifford Geertz has observed about normative beliefs in general, the law is a model *of* reality and model *for* reality.[31]

It is inaccurate and unhelpful, therefore, to conceive of this double-sided character of law in dualistic terms, as a matter of the absolute and the relative or the unconditional and the conditional. The absolute and unconditional are not some specific content apart from the particularity of the law, except in the most abstract sense that, as in the formal definition of justice, "each person should be given his or her due." The absolute and unconditional character of the law refers to the demand to acknowledge and care for the other as other. But this demand is known only in the particular, as the law demands some par-

29. See H. Richard Niebuhr, *The Responsible Self*, pp. 71-79.

30. Paul Ricoeur, *Oneself as Another*, trans. Kathleen Blamey (Chicago: University of Chicago Press, 1992), pp. 204-9.

31. Clifford Geertz, "Religion as a Cultural System," in *The Interpretation of Cultures: Selected Essays* (New York: Basic Books, 1973), pp. 126-41.

ticular action towards another and in the particular call heard in the actual meeting of another.

The moral tradition refers to the absolute and universal character of law as natural law or the divine law. This is the law of our nature, what makes humans human. Interpreted theologically, natural law is understood as given in relationship to God and hence in the divine law. In contrast, we live in a world of human or positive laws. These laws reflect the particular circumstances and understandings of a society. But, here again, these should not be conceived as two different sets of laws. Instead, they are two dimensions of law that we experience in the demands given socially. Interpreted by the law, we interpret the law. In the name of the meaning of the law, we challenge understandings of the law, reform the law, and extend the application of the law.[32] Such is at the heart of the vocation of the prophets, whether the eighth-century Hebrew prophets or twentieth-century prophets such as Mahatma Gandhi, Martin Luther King, or Desmond Tutu.

Justice as a matter of law is the form or the necessary condition for the realization of love. It is, however, never a final achievement. That is impossible given that justice as law is an abstraction from the encounter with the other. The relationship between love and justice is, therefore, best understood dialectically.[33] Love and justice presuppose each other, like a conversation, in a continual development, in what I have called the covenant of hospitality. The human hope for some final state in which love and justice are fully realized is one form of idealism. An idea is abstracted from the reality of life and projected as some ultimate, future state of affairs, as in popular notions of progress

32. Edward Farley, *Deep Symbols: Their Postmodern Effacement and Reclamation* (Valley Forge, Penn.: Trinity Press, 1996), pp. 74-84.

33. This is the fundamental insight developed by Reinhold Niebuhr. See *The Nature and Destiny of Man. Vol. II: Human Destiny* (New York: Charles Scribner's Sons, 1943), pp. 244-56. For Niebuhr, love is understood idealistically in terms of union related dialectically in time with justice. As hospitality, love is a dialectic between the recognition and the embrace of the other. Out of this dialectic of identity given in difference arises the dialectic between hospitality and justice.

or of heaven. Instead, the covenant of hospitality is a living reality and never dependent on some idea or future state of affairs. In this sense Christians have understood faith as an eschatological reality, experienced now but not yet, already even while not completely. Faith is quite simply a way of life, a practical piety, *in via,* on the way.

The moral dialectic between love and justice at the heart of the covenant of hospitality is understood religiously in terms of what has been called law and gospel. This distinction was made by the apostle Paul and developed, by the Protestant reformers, as expressing the center of Christian faith.[34] Law, on the one hand, refers to the particular demands of law: do this and do that; don't do this and don't do that. On the other hand, law is what the Jewish tradition calls Torah. Torah is not simply the law codes in the first five books of scripture but all that is in these books as they are the way of life that leads into God.[35] Paul and the Reformers name this way of life gospel. As such, gospel refers above all to the good news of Jesus Christ as the end or purpose and fulfillment of the law.

Given the ways in which law can become narrowly defined, gospel is then variously understood in order to point to the meaning of the law. As law is identified with the particular demands of the law, the gospel reveals that this life is nothing but faith active in love (Gal. 5:6). Instead of law, gospel is freedom (5:1). As people seek to achieve righteousness through the law — only to find themselves utterly unable to meet these demands — the gospel is spoken of as justification by grace through faith (Gal. 2:16). Gospel is always understood as the new life revealed and begun in Jesus, in his teaching, in the life lived in hospitality, and in the life given in death. Gospel refers then to the whole of this revelation. Sometimes this is identified with Paul's summary of

34. For a classic account of this distinction see Karl Barth, "Gospel and Law" in *Community, State and Church* (Gloucester, Mass.: Peter Smith, 1968), pp. 71-100.

35. See chapter one, pp. 9-11. For this broader discussion of law as a way of life which is a matter of love see Irving Singer's discussion of Judaism and *nomos* in *The Nature of Love. Vol. 1: Plato to Luther,* 2nd ed. (Chicago: University of Chicago Press, 1984), pp. 222-67. See also Farley, *Deep Symbols,* pp. 91-94.

the gospel, sometimes with the written gospels themselves, and sometimes simply by singular words: faith, Christ, the Way, the Truth, the Light, eternal life.

Like love and justice, gospel is not opposed to law but is the meaning of law as the way of life that reconciles division and gives wholeness to life. As this life is given as a living covenant, the gospel is not an end beyond the law. The gospel is realized, rather, in life lived out in the midst of the call of the other, as that call is given in the demand of the law. Law and gospel are dialectically related. The understandings of the law express and enable the recognition and embrace of the other. The welcoming embrace of each other in the covenant of hospitality, in turn, is the end of law and the beginning of the assessment and the extension of the law itself.

The Christian understanding of the covenant of hospitality reveals and enables living into that covenant, into what Christians say is the spirit and not the letter of the law. Christian faith is then a matter of revelation. That is to say, Christian faith is a matter of knowing what is at the heart of our lives. Such revelation comes only from the experience of hospitality and the claiming of that experience as that which gives life. The first question for the Christian life is not then "What should I do?" but "How can I know and come to live more fully into the presence of God?" This is the question of the church, of how a community can be a continuing revelation of God. More specifically for Christians, this is, as Edward Schillebeeckx phrases it, the question of how the church can be the sacrament of Christ in the world in order to bear witness to the presence of God and to enable and deepen that presence in our lives.[36] As a matter of practical piety, the question is, "What are the practices of faith that bear faith in the world?"

36. Schillebeeckx, *Christ: The Sacrament of the Encounter with God.*

[CHAPTER 5]

The Practices of Faith

~

IN TEACHING in church congregations, I have often asked two questions, "What has been most significant in your experience of worship, and what has been most difficult?" I have asked these questions to young and old, newcomers and old-timers, women and men, the sophisticated and unsophisticated. The answers have a common theme. Most persons say simply, "I somehow felt something holy, sacred, in being among other people worshiping, in the quiet and through the music. What is most difficult is keeping alive that initial experience. What is most difficult is making sense of what worship is all about." More broadly, what appears to be most difficult in keeping faith alive is moving from the initial experience of mystery, dependence, grace, and awe to connecting this experience to the rest of life.

While worship may offer the experience of the presence of God, the experience of worship is not itself the covenant of our lives. We come fully into the presence of God only as we are reconciled to all that constitutes life itself. And this is impossible unless the story of faith makes sense of our lives, so that the story told is the story lived. It is especially difficult for once-a-week worship to convey this larger reality instead of becoming a singular experience in itself.

In the early church the development of faith did not begin narrowly in worship but in joining a group of seekers, called *catecumen-*

ates, who were taught the story of faith as a way of life.[1] The word itself means those being instructed. Instruction in this case was not narrowly a matter of learning the story of faith. More broadly, to be instructed in Christian faith was to be instructed in a way of life. Since the world was viewed as fallen, turned away from the way of life revealed and begun in Jesus, faith depended on schooling people in an alternative community. Instruction in faith was learning an art, the art of living faithfully. Or to use another image, schooling was a matter of therapy, not individual therapy but social therapy.[2] In undertaking a set of disciplines individuals were freed from the constraints of a fallen world. A new life was experienced. In this way, as training in a way of life, the church formed disciples, followers of this way.

The disciplines central to instruction in Christian faith were distinctive in content but were the same kinds of disciplines that were developed in the philosophical schools of late antiquity. Broadly speaking, four types of disciplines may be identified, disciplines that have their beginning in Plato's academy in the early fourth century before the birth of Christianity. These disciplines may be designated meditation and contemplation, examination (as in the examination of our lives), denial and the simplification of life, and action.[3] Again, Christians adopted these disciplines for the same reason they were developed by the Greeks: a way of life is a matter of training.

1. On the catecumenate and its renewal see Michael W. Merriman, ed., *The Baptismal Mystery and the Catecumenate* (New York: Church Hymnal, 1990).

2. See Martha C. Nussbaum, *Therapy of Desire: Theory and Practice in Hellenistic Ethics* (Princeton, N.J.: Princeton University Press, 1994), pp. 13-47. See also Michel Foucault, "Technologies of the Self," in *Technologies of the Self: A Seminar with Michel Foucault,* ed. Luther H. Martin, Huck Gutman, and Patrick H. Hutton (Amherst, Mass.: University of Massachusetts Press, 1988), p. 31.

3. Pierre Hadot has analyzed the spiritual exercises in late antiquity in light of two lists of exercises from Philo of Alexandria. Pierre Hadot, *Philosophy as a Way of Life,* trans. Michael Chase (Oxford: Blackwell, 1995), pp. 81-109. The four (ideal-typical) types of disciplines designated here are an interpretation of the general features of these practices. On the Christian appropriation of these disciplines see pp. 126-40.

Disciplines of Mind and Body

Meditation and contemplation are disciplines of the mind. To meditate and contemplate is to attend to something and to hold it in consciousness, to dwell upon it and experience it in memory. Meditation and contemplation are a matter of focusing attention. As the schools of philosophy emphasized, without these disciplines we are forever reacting to whatever is the strongest impulse or anxiety. To meditate and contemplate is to become free from narrow captivity to social roles and expectations, from bondage to the immediate and ephemeral desires and pleasures of the present.

Meditation and contemplation are first of all grounded in images. Called *kataphatic,* a person holds in consciousness a single image or a series of images. For example, the Psalms provide a wealth of images that construe God — as rock, refuge, shield, and deliverer, but also as awesome, far away, beyond comprehension. More broadly, the reading of scripture, prayer, and worship are all occasions for meditation and contemplation. Reading scripture is itself an act of listening. In listening, the worshiper holds before him or herself an image in order to discern the presence of God or simply to taste and feel that presence. Similarly, in worship and prayer the Christian attends to the majesty and glory of God, the gifts of life as he or she understands them as given by God, and the realities of life as they open him or her to God. Cross, Bible, altar, windows, baptismal font, bread and wine, statuary, icons: the church as a place of worship is holy because it is a place where God is encountered in meditation and contemplation.

While images focus meditation and contemplation, they also limit the experience of God. Images always represent and so construe experience in one way rather than another. In this way the image becomes narrowly identified with God. The icon is liable to become idol. Iconoclasts, literally breakers of icons, react in order to return to the larger experience of God. Strategies have also developed in meditation and contemplation in order to free consciousness from bondage to the image. What are called imageless or *apophatic* forms of contemplation turn from the image in order to gain an immediate experience of the presence of Being, what mystics identify as God.[4] Centering prayer, for example, proceeds by the simple action of being fully attentive to the present. Focusing on a word or sound, images well up and then pass away from consciousness until there is the experience of presence itself.

What distinguishes prayer in Judaism and Christianity as a distinctive form of meditation and contemplation is its personal character. Jew and Christian address God personally as a matter of thanks, praise, repentance, and petition. Those in prayer stand in the presence of God, vulnerable and naked before God. They wait upon the Lord and ask for guidance and consolation. They confess their failings, their brokenness, and their distance from God. They call to God for help. Prayer is more than meditation and contemplation of an object. Prayer is more like a conversation. In prayer Christians are not philosophers but worshipers. In prayer they meditate and contemplate, question and are questioned, ask and receive, love and are loved, bless and are blessed. Personal language is the language of prayer. It alone expresses and effects the relationship that Christians experience in prayer.

As the ancients knew, meditation and contemplation on what is true, good, and beautiful cannot help but call into question the order and relationships of everyday life. There is no good for us apart from our relationship to it. We may contemplate the nature of love and justice, but what that means we can only know as we examine the relationships of our own lives. More broadly, the starry skies may be good and beautiful, worthy of contemplation. But to acknowledge such beauty is also to acknowledge how we are related to nature, to see, for example, that nature will continue beyond our individual aspirations and hopes and beyond our lives themselves. Reflection on nature cannot finally be separate from reflection on ourselves. Though distinct, meditation and contemplation go hand in hand with examination. As ancient philosophers said, "Meditation is the practice of dialogue with oneself."[5]

4. For an exploration of the nature of God in light of the *kataphatic* and *apophatic,* or what may be called the prophetic and mystic, see David Tracy, *Dialogue with the Other: The Inter-Religious Dialogue* (Grand Rapids: Eerdmans, 1991).

5. Hadot, p. 91.

Dialogue may be the most elemental form of examination. As exemplified in the Socratic dialogues, in conversation persons question each other and thereby come to question what they think and believe. Socrates asks, what is good or what is just, and the conversation begins. Initial convictions are questioned until an answer makes sense in general. Listening to a story or the reading of a text are similar forms of examination. In reading, for example, a person can only comprehend the words of a description or narrative when the words construe or refigure what he or she has experienced in his or her own life. In the reading of a text — perhaps a parable, a proverb, a prophetic oracle, or an extended narrative, whether historical or mythic — the reader examines his or her life as the text illumines and questions, extends and corrects what were otherwise taken-for-granted understandings.

Parables epitomize how hearing a story is a form of examination. The story of the Good Samaritan (Luke 10:25-37), for example, has two religiously observant Jews walk by a man who has been robbed, beaten, and left to die on the side of the road. The Samaritan responds by bandaging the wounded man, carrying him to an inn, caring for him, and then leaving the innkeeper two days' wages so that the wounded man can stay until he can be on his way. We have heard the story so often, or at least reference to the story, that we abstract and summarize the parable by saying we should likewise love our neighbor. But in the initial telling and effective retelling, the shock of the parable is not so much in the act of love as in who is in touch with God and how.[6] It is as if for us an outsider — whether that be the stockbroker, the gay man, the Navy commander, or the homeless woman — offered themselves unconditionally for another. The shock poses the question: "Who is it that is really is in touch with God?" And we cannot help but then examine ourselves with the questions: "How is it

6. The pioneering work on parables as offering a shock that transforms the reader is John Dominic Crossan, *In Parables: The Challenge of the Historical Jesus* (New York: Harper & Row, 1973). See also Crossan, *The Dark Interval: Towards a Theology of Story* (Niles, Ill.: Argus, 1975). This understanding of parables is developed as a model for theology by Sallie McFague (TeSelle), *Speaking in Parables: A Study in Metaphor and Theology* (Philadelphia: Fortress, 1975).

that we are or aren't in touch with God? How do our customs and religious practices become ends in themselves that isolate us like the observant Jews who walked by the stranger? How may we respond in order to deepen the covenant of life?"

The gospels as a whole effect the most radical questioning of the human person. The persistent call to awaken and turn from evil ways arises from the immediate sense of the presence of God. The kingdom of God is at hand, already now breaking in on the present. In order to respond, the gospels turn away from some external standard that could be calculated objectively. Instead of an economy of exchange, of offering good for good and returning evil for evil, an eye for an eye and a tooth for a tooth (Exod. 21:23-24; Lev. 24:19-20; Matt. 5:38), the gospels call for the whole person to desire the well-being of the other. Instead of an external law and order, an internal demand is given. Alms are not to be given openly where reward is gained but in secret. Prayers are not to be offered publicly before others but in secret. Fasting is not to become a public show but, again, should be done in secret. After each of these commands in the Gospel of Matthew, Jesus says, "Your Father who sees in secret will reward you" (Matt. 6:4b, 6b, 16b).

No matter what happens, the gospel questions the human person in all things in order that he or she will *will* one thing, the well-being of the other. An economy of sacrifice (of offering of oneself fully for the sake of the other) replaces the economy of exchange (of doing this for that). No longer are consequences the measure. All that matters is response because God is already present. We are, after all, fully present to God who "sees in secret."[7]

This radical questioning of the human person in the gospels leads to Augustine and the most radical method of self-examination, the confession.[8] In his *Confessions,* Augustine seeks to tell the story of

7. Jacques Derrida, *The Gift of Death,* trans. David Wills (Chicago: University of Chicago Press, 1995), pp. 101-9. "What is called God," says Derrida, "is in me, he is the absolute 'me' or 'self.' He is the structure of invisible interiority that is called, in Kierkegaard's sense, subjectivity" (p. 109).

8. Foucault, "Technologies of the Self," pp. 40-49. This was first argued by Charles Norris Cochrane, *Christianity and Classical Culture: A Study of Thought*

his life as the story of his desire by detailing the most particular events of his life. Whatever was done is told as either an expression of his deepest desire or else as rebellion, a turning away from that desire. All the events of a person's life are important. They form a story of desire. Each event, therefore, is to be questioned in order to discover what is truly desired. Examination thus leads to meditation and contemplation and, for Christians, to prayer. In more theological language, the practice of confession becomes a double confession: the confession of sin leads to a confession of faith.

Confessional practices have developed in a variety of ways. The confession of the self in therapy, journaling, intimate letters, and conversations among friends — all are confessional. In the church, specifically confessional practices include the examination of conscience and the confession of sin, conversations with spiritual friends or a spiritual director, guided meditations and directed retreats, devotional readings, and more generally fellowship formed around prayer, study, and support. Examination and prayer are always integrally related. The one leads into and supports the other.

The "intellectual exercises" of meditation, contemplation, and examination are ineffective without exercises of the body. The human self is always an embodied self, not a mind attached to a body but an embodied spirit. This is what is meant by saying that the human person is incarnate, literally enfleshed. The body is the self's opening to the world, the way by which the self is in touch, comes to know, and is known by others. Meditation and contemplation draw upon the experience of the body to hold before consciousness, through images or beyond images, the experience of what is true and enduring. Practical exercises are the more specific bodily disciplines that withdraw, intensify, or redirect the immediate experience of the body in order to deepen the experience of what is true and enduring.

These practical disciplines may be distinguished between acts of denial and simplification and acts that are, broadly speaking, sacra-

---

and Action from Augustus to Augustine (London: Oxford, 1940), pp. 386-96. Also see Albrecht Diehle, *The Theory of the Will in Classical Antiquity* (Berkeley: University of California Press, 1982), pp. 123-44.

mental. Acts of denial and simplification are traditionally called acts of purgation. These acts shape bodily desire through the denial or restriction of human actions. For example, the three most common, traditional acts of purgation are fasting, sexual renunciation, and bodily mortification. The second practical discipline was called by ancients "duties," but may be best understood as sacramental acts. Sacramental acts are actions that bring the person into direct experience of what is true and good. Table fellowship, welcoming the stranger, feeding the hungry, caring for the sick, visiting those in prison, and simply forgiving those who have acted against them — these stand out as examples of Christian sacramental acts.[9]

Acts of denial and simplification are not in themselves a matter of hating or destroying the body.[10] Instead, as disciplines of the spirit they are undertaken in order to enable persons to feel what is finally sustaining and enduring. In this sense, denial and simplification are forms of *ascesis*, a matter of disciplining the flesh so that the body may be whole. Fasting, for example, awakens hunger and the sense of taste so that food is appreciated anew as the staff of life and as delectable in both its simplicity and complexity. Voluntary hunger as well awakens the sense of our human frailty and dependence. The withdrawal of food is then a source for meditation and an examination of our dependencies, from those who grow food and prepare it to the hospitality that food offers. In this way, in fasting the body forms thought, reality is contemplated, life is examined, and all of this is experienced in the body as something more than a good idea.

Fasting, sexual renunciation, and bodily mortification may, and

9. As the distinctive practices of Christian faith, this list of sacramental acts is drawn from scripture (for example, Matt. 25:34-40) in light of the practices of the developing church. See Wayne Meeks, *The Origins of Christian Morality: The First Two Centuries* (New Haven, Conn.: Yale University Press, 1993), pp. 91-110; and Margaret R. Miles, *Practicing Christianity: Critical Perspectives for an Embodied Spirituality* (New York: Crossroad, 1990), pp. 114-25.

10. Kallistos Ware, "The Way of the Ascetics: Negative or Affirmative?" *Asceticism*, ed. Vincent L. Wimbush and Richard Valantasis (New York: Oxford, 1995), pp. 3-13.

often have, become narrowly focused on the negation of the body itself. When this happens asceticism becomes what is called rigorist. The true self is conceived as separate from an evil body. The good is measured by the severity of bodily negation. If fasting for a day is good, then a week-long fast is better. Rigorism is usually opposed by calls for freedom from body-denying disciplines. Discipline and freedom, however, are falsely placed in opposition. Denial and simplification may rather be undertaken in order to free the self to act in accord with its deepest desire. The question of any ethic is what kinds of disciplines are needed in order to shape the self into a unified body connected to what is enduring.[11]

Contemporary culture has been variously described as a consumer culture, a culture of desire, a culture of narcissism, and a therapeutic culture.[12] What this means is that the human self is formed in its desires by images that are increasingly disconnected from a deeper set of relationships given, for example, in family, culture, nation, and religion. In a fragmented world the self is fragmented, no longer connected by a web of relationships. Instead, a person feels alive only in the experience of the immediate present. In such a society, everything is reduced to the promise of pleasure and fulfillment. Images become all-consuming. Style is everything. In a consumer culture, denial of something is necessary in order for the self to be anything other than the conclusion of a series of advertising stimuli. To have a self, a new asceticism must be developed.

This brings us to the second kind of practical disciplines. Ancients referred to these as accomplishment of duties. They are acts of obligation in the sense that they express the bond and in turn bind us to what is

11. For a reading of the Christian tradition in terms of rigorism and the reaction to rigorism, see Kenneth E. Kirk, *The Vision of God* (London: Longmans, Green and Co., 1932).

12. See Stuart Ewen, *All Consuming Images: The Politics of Style in Contemporary Culture* (New York: Basic Books, 1988); Christopher Lasch, *The Culture of Narcissism: American Life in an Age of Diminishing Expectations* (New York: Norton, 1978); Philip Rief, *The Triumph of the Therapeutic: Uses of Faith after Freud* (New York: Harper & Row, 1966).

good and enduring. They also may be called sacramental acts. As sacramental, these acts mark where and how God is present as they deepen the sense of that presence in those who undertake these acts.

The greatest influences in the formation of the human self are the roles and relationships of family, culture, and society. While an individual is formed by these roles and relationships, he or she never responds only out of a particular role. In the midst of roles the human person acts in light of his or her convictions regarding what is judged to be good, right, and worthy. Sacramental acts are then those actions undertaken beyond what is done narrowly as a matter of social role in the family, as an economic producer, or as a citizen. Welcoming the stranger, feeding the hungry, caring for the sick, visiting those in prison, forgiving those who have acted against us, and, perhaps most prosaically but fundamentally, sharing meals together in table fellowship — in these actions Christians claim they experience the full presence of God in a way that orients or reorients, forms or transforms, the roles and relations of everyday life.

The regular exercise of these sacramental acts may appear to be the conclusion of the Christian life. However, to view a set of acts as the end or conclusion of the Christian life is to misunderstand the nature of spiritual disciplines. For example, as a spiritual discipline, the decision to work in the garden or to serve meals at the soup kitchen is not an action that is chosen for what will be accomplished in some grand scheme of things, as if the purpose were to bring in the kingdom of God. If that were the case, persons might accomplish far more in the variety of roles they have, as teachers, carpenters, plumbers, bankers, lawyers, farmers, parents, and citizens. Instead of seeking some extrinsic end, sacramental acts are done in and of themselves because they are the embrace of God. Instead, above all, sacramental acts enable persons to know, claim, and deepen where and how they are connected to God and the good in their daily lives.

In a well-ordered society all the practices forming the full experience of the good would be part of the fabric of society, so much so that little thought would be given to them.[13] Few explicit spiritual disci-

13. Nussbaum, pp. 96-101.

plines would be necessary because the practices that form daily life would provide a unified way of life in which human desire is focused and integrated, for example, in the spheres of family and friends, work, and politics. The transcendence gained in spiritual exercises would, moreover, be part of taken-for-granted practices.

For example, listening to the stories of elders and learning to tell stories would provide a regular opportunity for both contemplation and examination and a kind of personal participation that may be best described as prayer and worship. Living in a place at the cross of cultures, the metropolis, persons might regularly sit, eat, and talk with others who are both like themselves and different. They would learn how to listen and hear persons who challenge their world and draw them out into a broader respect and care for others. In this way hospitality would simply be part of their lives.

The contemporary, postmodern world, however, is fragmented. It lacks practices that bring the person into the relationships that give unity and wholeness to all of life. Instead, daily disciplines are more likely to be part of an enclave shaped narrowly by a therapeutic culture. This is particularly evident in persons who have come into adulthood since the late 1970s and early 1980s. This generation has been called the "X generation" (X for unknown, hidden, or disconnected). Many "X-ers" and others have elaborate disciplines centered on electronic communications. One "X-er" described his first daily discipline after waking up as calling someone on the telephone. "I just have to talk to someone when I get up or I don't feel alive." Others wake up, tune into a radio or CD, plug in earphones, pull out cellular phones, check their e-mail, or browse the Internet. Such disciplines are elaborate and time-consuming. They connect disparate individuals to others, but there is no larger, shared world.

The self-conscious development of spiritual disciplines in late antiquity arose in a world that was also fragmented. Christians adopted and transformed these disciplines as they sought to establish a unified life in Christ. Similarly in the present, postmodern world of competing interests, Christian faith depends on the development of spiritual disciplines. An exclusive focus on disciplines, however, will narrow and distort Christian faith by identifying faith with a particular practice. For example, a focus on centering prayer and other contemplative practices may create an experience of unity but that unity will not be in relationship to the larger world. As has been the case for many Christian ascetics, the experience of wholeness is given by assuming a dichotomy between body and soul and then denying the one in order to form an idealized experience of the other. Such is not an ultimate unity or wholeness, not what I have called a covenant of life or, more specifically, the covenant of hospitality.

At different times and places in our lives different disciplines will likely be more needed and hence emphasized. For example, the intellectual disciplines of meditation, contemplation, and examination may be especially needed at times of transition or when the demands of daily life threaten to altogether define our lives. Times of major commitments — for example, a decision to marry or to become a member of a community — require examination, a reflecting on what is good and central to one's own life. At other times, the need to center and form life may focus on the disciplines of the body. Those living and working among like-minded, relatively affluent people, for example, have a particular need for self-conscious disciplines of hospitality. Tutoring or visiting the sick may be important disciplines that can draw the well established out into covenant with the larger human community. Such acts of service are sacramental acts. In turn, they may need to be developed in tandem with a certain simplification of life.

Worship and the Disciplines of Faith

For all Christians, the disciplines of Christian faith are centered in worship. Worship is first of all a matter of prayer. More broadly, though, worship incorporates all four of the disciplines of formation: meditation and contemplation, examination, denial and simplification, and symbolic acts. The distinctive Christian content of worship is expressed in what is variously called Holy Eucharist, the Lord's Supper, or Holy Communion.

As a matter of meditation and contemplation, the Eucharist is centered in Jesus' command to his disciples to eat the Passover bread and wine with the words, "This is my body that is for you. Do this in remembrance of me, and this cup is the new covenant in my blood. Do this, as often as you drink it, in remembrance of me" (1 Cor. 11:24-25 and in the synoptic gospels Mark 14:22-24; Matt. 26:26-28; Luke 22:19-20). A meal of bread and wine, the Eucharist is also a reenactment of the passion and commendation of Jesus' life into God.[14] In this way Christians meditate and contemplate the truth of Jesus' words and actions centered on the Last Supper and his suffering and death by crucifixion. At the same time, Eucharistic worship is a matter of examination. Worshipers examine their own lives in light of this paschal mystery. They discern how they are and are not in Christ.

More than intellectual disciplines, the Eucharist is also an action of denial and simplification. Traditionally, Christians fasted before Eucharist. They ate nothing from midnight until the Eucharist Sunday morning. Moreover, as simply a matter of worship, Eucharist is time set apart. The daily structure of life is set aside, in one sense denied, in order to lay bare the worshiper before God. The physical act of worship itself purges desires and gives rise to the experience of dependence, that the self is not self-sufficient. In this sense Eucharist is an act that is traditionally called purgation. This is not absolute negation. Denial opens the self to the experience of transcendence given in the Eucharist.

Finally, as sacrament the experience of God in Eucharist is given not as an idea but in the action itself. The Eucharistic meal is first of all a matter of the gifts of nature, bread and wine. Bread of life, fruit of the vine, together they mark the earth and all that gives and sustains life. Food feeds the body. Wine quenches thirst. In this sense, the Eucharist is the experience of bodily sustenance. Second, more than bodily sustenance alone, Eucharist is the experience of table fellow-

14. This is the central claim of sacramental theologies beginning with Edward Schillebeeckx, *Christ: The Sacrament of the Encounter with God,* trans. Paul Barrett (New York: Sheed and Ward, 1963). See David N. Power, *Unsearchable Riches: The Symbolic Nature of the Liturgy* (New York: Pueblo, 1984), pp. 196-205.

ship. In eating and drinking together worshipers come together in the welcoming embrace of hospitality. They have communion. Third, bread and wine are for Christian worshipers the body and blood of Jesus Christ. With this identification, the breaking of the bread and the sharing of a cup of wine become a sharing in the Last Supper. The bread and wine of this Jewish Passover meal is taken as Jesus' body and blood. The Eucharistic life is the life of Christ, a matter of dying and being raised into God.[15]

Something of the range of meanings brought together in the Eucharist is summarized in the common statement from the World Council of Churches on baptism, Eucharist, and ministry.[16] First, the Eucharist is a common meal of thanksgiving for everything that is, an offering and hymn of praise and thanksgiving. Second, the Eucharistic thanksgiving is grounded in Jesus' life, his ministry and teaching, as they culminate in his death and resurrection. Life in its entirety is a life of death and resurrection. In the Eucharist, Christians reenact this life of Jesus offering himself to God in thanksgiving. In this sense, Eucharist is what in Greek is called *anamnesis,* what is translated as something done "in memory" but may be better understood as reenactment.

Third, Eucharist is an invocation of the Spirit. As the offering of one's whole life in thanksgiving, the offering is an invocation, the calling of God to be present. Since God is for Christians the power that is the good of life, to call for God's presence is to call for blessing. Fourth, the Eucharist is the blessing itself. What is asked is received. As such, the fifth and final image or understanding of Eucharist expressed in this common statement is that of eschatological feast. Eucharist is the celebration and foretaste of the meal of the kingdom in which all the world is reconciled.

The play of metaphors in the Eucharist extends meanings by

15. Sacramental theologies of the Eucharist focus on these layers of meaning. See, for example, David Power, *Unsearchable Riches,* and Gordon H. Lathrop, *Holy Things: A Liturgical Theology* (Minneapolis: Fortress, 1993).

16. World Council of Churches, *Baptism, Eucharist and Ministry* (Switzerland: World Council of Churches, 1982), pp. 10-17.

joining together what would otherwise appear to be disconnected: breaking and blessing, death and life, cross and resurrection. As bread and wine are taken and blessed, broken and shared, all of life is a matter of a gift taken up, broken, and shared. This is a way of life that stands in contrast and resistance to the way of the world. In this way is the blessing and thanksgiving of life. In this is the participation and raising up of life into God. Life is like bread and wine. Jesus is the bread of life. Bread is the body of life. Broken, this is the bread of heaven. Jesus' blood is wine. Shed, this wine is the cup of salvation.

Any single image that seeks to convey the meaning of the Eucharist is inadequate. As the image draws together some features, it abstracts from others. Last Supper refers to Jesus' last meal, his celebration of the Jewish Passover with his disciples. Agape meal more broadly construes table fellowship as expressing the meaning of love. Holy Communion draws together the meaning of this celebration as that which brings us into relationship to God. More broadly still, the Eucharist conveys that this worship is a matter of thanksgiving. Still other terms used to image the Eucharist include Mass, sacrifice, and paschal mystery. Drawn from the Latin words concluding the service of worship, the Roman Catholic Church has called this worship the Mass, literally meaning to dismiss or to send out. The Eucharist is thus construed in terms of service. More conceptually, the Eucharist is a holy sacrifice and a paschal mystery.

To many people, this final image of Eucharist as sacrifice is the most problematic image. In common usage sacrifice means to give up oneself for another. To admonish the poor and oppressed to turn the other cheek, to love their enemies and those who hate them, to bless those who are reviled, and to promise that in so doing their reward will be great (Luke 6:22-35) is to place sacrifice at the center of life. For women, slaves, and others who are subordinate to those in power, such a way of life threatens the loss of self. This is so not simply because of the individual consequences; all life involves care for others and, in that sense, the sacrifice of narrowly defined interests. However, to bless sacrifice unconditionally is to bless the present order of things, to consecrate the hierarchy of dominance and subservience. The consequence of such a blessing is to define the oppressed in their roles as subordinate, of less value, as not full participants in human life.[17]

The woman lives for her man and her children. There may be in these relationships love and care, but there is also inequality. Sometimes this inequality is relatively benign. Often, however, it is brutish at best and too often brutal. Women have born the burden of child care and the unending work of sustaining the household — meals, gathering supplies, preparing meals, washing dishes, cleaning clothes, and caring for the sick. They have as well been subject to violence, verbal harangues, beatings, and rape. Moreover, in sacrificing themselves, women imprint on the next generation of women the same role, a role that accepts and in accepting enables continued violence towards women.

The word *sacrifice* may have become univocal in its meaning. It may be that to hear the word *sacrifice* will now only be understood in the sense of giving up oneself, of abandoning oneself and so violating one's integrity. The meaning of sacrifice, however, is more complex and indicates why the Eucharist has been called a holy sacrifice and, in turn, the paschal mystery.[18] The word *sacrifice* itself comes from the Latin *sacrificium* which means to make something sacred. In this sense, sacrifice was associated with an offering to the gods. This offering was often that of an animal, hence the phrase "a blood sacrifice" and hence the identification of sacrifice with killing something for someone else. What was offered to the gods was then accepted and made holy, filled with divine power. To the extent that the gods were good, acknowledging the gods in the offering of sacrifice was a form of thanksgiving for both what was and what was to be. Sacrifice was in this regard not narrowly a matter of giving something for someone else but a gift or a thank offering to the gods. Of course, the association of sacrifice with gaining favor and blessing was never far behind. Still,

17. Rosemary Radford Reuther, *Sexism and God-Talk* (Boston: Beacon, 1983), pp. 79-80; Miles, pp. 99-102.

18. See Lathrop, pp. 139-58. For my own earlier development of such an understanding, see Timothy F. Sedgwick, *Sacramental Ethics: Paschal Identity and the Christian Life* (Philadelphia: Fortress, 1987), pp. 38-52.

the meaning of sacrifice was broader than giving something in order to get something back, much less the simple identification of sacrifice with loss.

The broader understanding of sacrifice as offering and thanksgiving is above all connected for the Jewish people with the Exodus, with their own history in becoming a people: going down to Egypt during the time of great famine, suffering slavery, finding freedom in their exodus into the desert, and from all this called to be a new kind of people who settled a new land and formed a nation, but always with a larger sense that life was given in the welcome embrace and care for the stranger and those in need (Deut. 26:1-11). As the story of Exodus is told, this transformation of the Hebrew people is not a human triumph but a divine act. God has the Israelites make sacrifice by having each house offer a lamb to God, but first drawing the blood of the lamb and marking the doorposts of their houses with that blood. Their liberation then came when God smote the firstborn of the Egyptians but not those of the Israelites. They acknowledged God and, in turn, God passed over their houses marked by the blood of the lamb. They were thus given freedom, sent out to become a different kind of people, a people who knew that God was in the face of the poor and oppressed.

For the Jewish people, the Exodus connects the meaning of sacrifice to that of Passover or what is called *Pasch* and for Christians comes to be called the paschal mystery. The Exodus itself transformed the offering of first fruits of the harvest. Instead of first fruits, the Jewish people sacrifice food that their ancestors had eaten on that last night before God passed over them. This is the Passover feast, now reenacted in remembrance and thanksgiving. As reenactment, the Passover feast, now called the Seder, is the renewed offering of these worshipers to God, a matter of entrusting themselves to a new future grounded in resistance to oppression. In this sense, the Israelites then and the Jewish people now offer their lives for the sake of freedom. This sacrifice cannot be misunderstood as a submission that consecrates dominance. Sacrifice is tied to resistance to evil given in entrusting oneself beyond oneself in the embrace and care of the oppressed. In this sacrifice the Israelites are passed over into God.

Christians draw on these rich meanings that were connected to *sacrifice* and extend them still further. For Christians, Jesus is the true sacrifice in that he offers his whole life to God in resisting evil and embracing the other. He gives himself to God fully, in trust and thanksgiving. Here is the full revelation that the economy of life is that of sacrifice and not an economy of exchange. Life is given in hospitality for no reason beyond that embrace. Hence the Lord's Prayer begins, "Our Father in heaven, hallowed be your name, your kingdom come, your will be done."

The full revelation of this faith culminates in Jesus' suffering and death. Here is revealed that all of life is given up to God, entrusted in the covenant of hospitality. "Into your hands O Lord, I commend my spirit" (Luke 23:46). This leads to the final word used to name the Eucharist. As the word for Passover is Pasch, Jesus is called the true paschal lamb and the Eucharist is called the paschal mystery. As reenacted in the Eucharist, life is given in the sacrifice of Jesus. In this sacrifice Christians are passed over into God. In sacrifice we pass into God; in losing ourselves we gain new life. We move from death to life; in and through the cross we are resurrected, literally raised into or passed over into God.[19]

For many of us today, unlike the Jews and pagans of late antiquity, the rich associations of *sacrifice* may be unavailable. When that happens — as is the case for those who have been "sacrificed" for the benefit of others — the gospel is neither spoken nor heard in the language of sacrifice. To say that Jesus sacrificed himself for our sake on the hard wood of the cross or that Jesus died for our sins is then anathema to the gospel. Resignation at best and self-hatred at worst replaces the freedom given in the covenant of hospitality claimed in resistance to injustice. The problem of language is that the same words mean different things to different people, given their differences in experience and associations. Worship, and the Eucharist in particular, cannot,

19. See Karl Rahner, "The Eucharist and Suffering," *Theological Investigations. Vol. 3,* trans. Karl-H. and Boniface Kruger (London: Darton, Longman & Todd, 1967), pp. 161-70.

therefore, have one single form if by that is meant an identical worship in all matters of words and actions.

True worship of God is not a particular form of worship but an offering of the self to God. This is the case whether worship is a solemn, sung Eucharist or a service of prayer and praise. In black churches, for example, spirituals and blues are forms of prayer that in their concreteness enable worshipers to name the evils and restraints that hold them captive. Song, moreover, enables them to call out for deliverance and freedom from their sufferings. Calling to Jesus, worshipers commend themselves to God. In this action they are drawn beyond themselves to where they see and taste a new and promised land.[20] A sermon likewise may begin as a telling and retelling of the story of scripture in our own time, but it moves into prayer as the preacher leads the congregation in a series of responsive prayers that conclude with the worshipers commending themselves to God. Such worship is true worship, as much or even more than a Eucharist itself may be.

Whatever the form of worship, the danger in worship for Christians is that the particular form of worship does not recollect the story of Christ in such a way as to enable the reenactment of that faith and the offering of life in God. When this fails to happen, worship becomes an enclave separated from the rest of life. Worship may then entertain through stories and music. Worship may function aesthetically as a dramatic, musical performance. Worship may function socially as the place to gather for fellowship, to confirm social roles and relations, and to socialize children and outsiders into a community. However, worship is an idol unless it is the reenactment of faith as commendation of the human person in the covenant of hospitality.

20. For such an account of spirituals and blues see Riggins Earl, *Dark Symbols, Obscure Signs: God, Self, and Community in the Slave Mind* (Maryknoll, N.Y.: Orbis, 1993).

Hospitality and Forgiveness

Dietrich Bonhoeffer was acutely aware of how Christian worship became idolatrous. Ultimately hanged by the Nazis for his role in a failed attempt to kill Hitler, Bonhoeffer believed that the churches of Germany had prevented rather than enabled a living faith among the German people. Worship and preaching had become self-referential. Christians referred to themselves so that salvation was separate from the world. Consequently, the churches uncritically supported the government, the Third Reich, as ordained by God. In this way, ordinary people came to be collaborators in the Jewish Holocaust. Christian faith, said Bonhoeffer, was captive to religion, to an institutional reality; hence, he called for a "nonreligious" interpretation of Christianity.[21]

In order to experience and respond to the presence of God, Bonhoeffer sought an integral relationship between worship and the world. Drawing from his experience in religious communities, Bonhoeffer emphasized the need for the development of daily prayer and the reading of scripture, solitude and silence, corporate prayer and singing, sharing in meals together, confession and forgiveness, and the celebration together of the Lord's Supper.[22] These disciplines celebrate as they form the Christian in a way of life in the world that is not of the world or captive to the world. The end, though, is never the religious community but response to God in the daily life of the world. What Bonhoeffer knew was that without the practices of faith persons are lost in the roles, demands, and expectations given in the world about them. Worship then becomes "religion." Instead, to be faithful, what is said and done in the community of faith must be a sign of how

21. Dietrich Bonhoeffer, *Letters and Papers from Prison,* ed. Eberhard Bethge (London: SCM, 1976), pp. 152-54.

22. See Dietrich Bonhoeffer, *Life Together,* trans. John W. Doberstein (New York: Harper & Row, 1954). For a contemporary constructive proposal for church and society drawing on Bonhoeffer, see Larry L. Rasmussen, *Moral Fragments and Moral Community: A Proposal for Church in Society* (Minneapolis: Fortress, 1993), pp. 165-67.

in our daily lives God is present and hence draws us into life in the world, what I have called the covenant of hospitality.

As an eschatological reality, the covenant of hospitality is experienced already but not yet, in part but not fully. That is why spiritual disciplines are developed: to deepen the experience of what is true and holy so that what is lived in part may be lived more fully. From the underside, spiritual disciplines are developed in order to combat sin. That is why they are exercises. They are intended to strengthen the human person in his or her capacity to abide in the covenant of hospitality. However, as a covenant, a relationship, the individual does not have the power within him or herself to establish the relationship in the first place. Instead, a covenant happens between persons and so requires a letting go of oneself in order to allow another person in. The spiritual disciplines are such a letting go. As true in prayer as in table fellowship, spiritual disciplines are, in this sense, acts of hospitality, a welcoming of another and entrusting oneself to another.

While appropriating the spiritual disciplines of the Hellenistic schools of philosophy in late antiquity, Christian spiritual disciplines are distinctively Christian as acts of hospitality. Contemplation and meditation are transformed into prayer as a matter of personal address and commendation to God. Examination is transformed from detailing of goals and failings to confession as a form of prayer in which sorrow leads to the call for forgiveness and the opening of the self to a new life. The simplification of life — whether in specific acts of self-denial or in a change in lifestyle — is a form of poverty, of becoming naked before God in order to feel and hear the presence of God beyond the constraints and comforts that distance and separate us from the world. Closely tied to simplification are specific acts of hospitality in which the other is welcomed and embraced, for example, in visiting the sick, caring for those in need, table fellowship, and forgiveness. Christian spiritual disciplines become practices of piety in that they invite and welcome the presence of God.

Of these Christian practices of hospitality, none is more central to the Christian life than forgiveness. Forgiveness has too often been narrowly understood in individual terms as a matter of releasing the individual from judgment. This reflects the origin of the word as pardoning a criminal for an offense or similarly letting go the debt someone owes. In this sense forgiveness is a letting go of a claim against another. However, forgiveness is ultimately a matter of restoring a relationship. To forgive is not only a letting go of a claim against another but doing so without resentment. Claims and counterclaims are built into all relationships. Marriage, friendship, sports, education, business, all designate relationships built on mutual expectations and, in turn, responsibilities. I do this for you and you do that for me. Together we share in life's projects, from securing the provisions for life to playing together. Failure to meet commitments is to fail to meet the legitimate claims we have on each other. Such failure is cause for not only disappointment and sorrow but for frustration and anger. Forgiveness in this context arises because we experience the power and goodness of the relations that draw us beyond ourselves and beyond claims and counterclaims. This is as true in the political relationship between oppressed and oppressor as in the personal relationship between friends and lovers.

At the heart of forgiveness is a twofold movement of repentance. First, forgiveness requires sorrow arising from the knowledge of separation and of fault. Knowledge of sin is the knowledge of how a person has failed to enter into the covenant of hospitality, of what has been done and what has been left undone. Beginning in confession and sorrow, a penitent is left alone before God, naked just like the poor and the ascetic. Stripped of his or her illusions of self-sufficiency, the true penitent is absolutely vulnerable. The prayer for forgiveness is the call for recognition and relationship that will bless life beyond merit and judgment. The experience of forgiveness is just such an experience, that which I have called by way of analogy the welcoming embrace of hospitality. In this sense, forgiveness is the grace that reveals the ultimate power and goodness of God.[23]

Forgiveness is not uniquely Christian. Given human failings,

23. See Nathan Mitchell, "Conversion and Reconciliation in the New Testament" and "The Table of Eucharist: Christian Fellowship and Christian Forgiveness," *The Rite of Penance. Vol. 3: Commentaries,* ed. Nathan Mitchell (Washington, D.C.: The Liturgical Conference, 1978), pp. 6-19, 62-72.

human relations depend on forgiveness. What is distinctive about the Christian life, however, is that forgiveness is not a matter of usefulness but a matter of goodness. For Christians, the embrace of the other is an embrace beyond claim and counterclaim. Life is given in this embrace of those both near and far, neighbor and stranger. Revealed most fully in Christ as known in Word and sacrament, the experience of forgiveness enables us to forgive. In forgiving we then commend ourselves back to God and enter more deeply into the covenant of hospitality. The grace of forgiveness is what connects the work of God and hospitality, what in the Ten Commandments are the two tables of the law, love of God and love of neighbor.

Like most older worshipers with whom I have talked, who have worshiped for the better part of their lives, I find that prayer and worship have their seasons. As a teaching member of a seminary community, for 20 years my own worship has been formed by a regular routine of daily worship. In my first year, like almost every first-year student, I was drawn out of myself by the round of worship and felt an exuberant joy. I felt in touch with God, with the community, with myself, and with the world about me. In time, given the routine, worship became a tedium. Worship seemed self-absorbed. At such times, worship was an obstacle to the vivid sense of the presence of God. Worship cast shadows instead of light, and I had some sense of what religious and mystics speak about as "the dark night of the soul." The vital connection to my life and to the world was cut off.

I suppose I have been fortunate; the changing seasons of worship have been for me marked by months rather than years. Perhaps it is my connection to the lives of the many members of the seminary community and to people outside the immediate community where I live. From these relationships to strangers, growing through specific commitments of service apart from the work of my job, I have come to a more vivid sense of the presence of God. Worship then returns to marking and celebrating a life lived, and so I am drawn into the other seasons of worship marked variously by wonder and surprise, care and compassion, forgiveness and forgiving, praise and thanksgiving.

By the end of each summer, just before the scattered seminary community gathers again to begin a new year, I am aware of how worship is central to my own life as a Christian. If I didn't have regular disciplines of reading scripture, quiet and listening, prayer and examination, I would have to "invent" them. I am then aware of how much I take for granted the disciplines of faith. In turn, I am aware how little most people are aware of such disciplines. The conclusion I draw is that the disciplines of faith, what were traditionally called spiritual exercises, need to be taught and discussed as central to the Christian life. I am also aware that the only language by which to make sense of this life is personal language. This is a life lived in response to God. Through the disciplines of faith this life is renewed and opened up. God embraces, calls, and invites me to a newness of life in the old and in the new. In this sense, the Christian life can only be adequately expressed and understood in the personal language of vocation, as a matter of calling and response. This brings us to the concluding chapter of this introduction to the Christian life.

CHAPTER 6

The Call of God

~

THE MOST important decisions in my own life have not been rational moral judgments about what I should do. The most important decisions have always been out of the ordinary. Marriage was a decision to form a life together, but it was clearly more a response to falling in love, and it has led me far beyond what I could have imagined. To teach at a seminary made sense to me, but the choice was still more like the acceptance of an invitation to a dinner party than the assumption of specific duties and tasks for which I was trained. Similarly, children were a choice but hardly a rational one, less a having and more a receiving of two guests. And the decision to have a friend and priest dying of AIDS live with us was again less a judgment that made sense and more a response that was simply called for.

My life decisions, large and small, cannot be understood in themselves as rational moral choices. Instead, the most important decisions in my life have been responses to limitations and openings that make sense only as responses to some call that I have heard as an invitation to enter further into a way of life which I have called hospitality. These decisions have not been narrowly moral decisions in the sense of acting to realize what is good or honor what is right. The decisions were of another order. Only the language of call and response seems adequate to describe them. As a Christian I can only say that my decisions are responses to the call of God — sometimes experienced as invitation and sometimes as demand, sometimes as judgment but always as grace.

The personal language of God is necessary to express the Christian understanding of our life.[1] We are judged. We are embraced and welcomed. We are loved. Impersonal language would simply not adequately comprehend our experience. This life is not a matter of some law discovered or given. The life that finally connects us is like an invitation. Life comes from beyond life as we know it. We are called to share in a new life. Again, the language of invitation, the language of call and response, is the only adequate way for Christians to articulate their experience. In this sense, the Christian life is to be understood as vocation.

The Nature of Calling

The word *vocation* comes from the Latin and literally means "calling."[2] Despite common usage, vocation is distinct from work. Work is laboring for some purpose or end. We do a day's work. She took on extra work to pay for her children's education. Vocation, on the other hand, is something we do in response to what we experience as a call or invitation. I am called to be a teacher, a nurse, a parent, an engineer, a musician, a social worker. I have felt the call to open my own business — a restaurant, a bike store, a fabric and yarn store. I am called to public service, to serve on the school board, or to work in the community shelter for the homeless. In each case, whether or not the means of earning money, vocation is a response to some larger sense of things.

1. See H. Richard Niebuhr, *Faith on Earth: An Inquiry into the Structure of Human Faith,* ed. Richard R. Niebuhr (New Haven, Conn.: Yale University Press, 1989), pp. 83-101.

2. For a summary of the history of understandings of vocation see Paul D. Holland, "Vocation," *The New Dictionary of Theology,* ed. Joseph Komonchak, Mary Collins, and Dermot A. Lane (Wilmington, Del.: Michael Glazier, 1987), pp. 1087-92.

The question of vocation is the question of this larger sense of things. More practically, the question of vocation is how to hear a call in the midst of the often confining situations in which we find ourselves — too busy and too tired to hear anything but the immediate demands of the moment.

For Christians work is always more than necessity, though it is that too. At the same time, work is not itself the source of meaning and fulfillment. Instead, work is given as necessity and opportunity where we may be called beyond ourselves into a covenant of hospitality. Two points are important to note. First, work is not the place of salvation. We must not fall victim to a "works righteousness" or what we more commonly know as workaholism. Nothing expresses this more clearly than the Ten Commandments, in which life together is given before God through honoring the Sabbath in worship. Second, vocation is more than work. We must be about more than making provision for ourselves. The problem of vocation is then broadened from what shall I do in order to make a living to, "What is it that God is calling me out of and into?" The spiritual question is not far behind: "How is it that we can hear and respond to God's call, not as something given in accepting a job but daily in what we do?"[3]

Historically, the problem of discerning God's call in daily life is posed between care for the world order and the renunciation of world maintenance in the immediate embrace of the stranger and those in need. This, of course, is the tension between those who would marry and raise a family and those who would assume sexual celibacy and form a community of prayer and hospitality apart from the bonds tying one generation to the next. This is also the problem of discerning God's call in the tension between property and poverty or between the use of force in world maintenance and the renunciation of force in nonviolent Christian pacifism. The danger of the one is identifying God's call with the world order, consecrating or sacralizing a particu-

---

3. Theologies of vocation in this sense as calling beyond the roles and relations given in society are, for reasons indicated below, limited. Most significant to my thought has been Karl Barth, *Church Dogmatics* III/4 (Edinburgh: T. & T. Clark, 1961), pp. 595-647.

lar people and their way of life apart from the larger world. The danger of the other is escape from the world into a compensatory world of the spirit, supported by a culture of its own, spiritualized instead of incarnate in the larger world.

The struggle to make sense of God's calling is the history of the church. "Render unto Caesar what is Caesar's and unto God what is God's" (Matt. 22:21; Mark 12:17; Luke 20:25) raises the question of what God is calling us to do but does not provide a simple answer. The answers Christians have given change as Christians' relationship to the world changes. In the midst of these answers we may hear what is at the heart of God's call.

In the early church, when the church was more an itinerant movement following on Jesus' death and resurrection, vocation as God's calling was synonymous with discipleship, with following in Jesus' way and life. Christians were to proclaim the faith in telling the story of God's work in Christ and in living that faith in the embrace and care of those in need. Daily work was a necessity to survive; but work was placed in the larger context of the community. Paul in his letters to the Corinthians pictures this Christian community as it ought to be. Each individual is part of the whole with distinctive gifts that when shared in love bind the individual into the body of Christ. Work is a necessity, but more; through work we share in a common life in which we come to know the love and care that we can only describe as the work of God's grace among us.

By the fourth century, Christianity became established as the religion of the Roman state. Christians were accordingly established; they were citizens of the state. The question of vocation, of God's calling, became established as well. This establishment reached its height in the feudal order of the Middle Ages. All persons were assumed to have a station in life, each with duties and privileges that complemented those of others, all for the good of the community as a whole. These stations were given by birth and consecrated in the socialization given in child rearing. Who you were was given by birth. You became who your parents were. Your duty was to live out that life in service to the larger community; hence, the virtues commended were especially humility and charity. Humility was a matter of accepting one's place in the social order in order to support the established order. Charity expressed the purpose of one's life, to be of service to others within the divinely established order.

In this feudal order, stations in life were given, naturally, in the course of birth. These positions were not considered vocations in the sense of being called out to serve God in some new way. Vocation as calling referred more narrowly to the religious call. Knighthood could also be appropriately understood as a vocation. In both cases, persons were called to an "extra-ordinary" task outside or beyond their station in life. For the soldier, this call was to strengthen the established order by defending the church and state from those who might threaten it from without and from within. This often meant Muslims, witches, and Jews.

The religious call was itself twofold: to serve the church as clergy or to become a member of a religious community. Clergy were called from the family to the church. Their task was to establish faith through their work for the church. In this way they were also called to establish the church. The call to religious was different. They were called more narrowly to lives of prayer and hospitality. Ascetics, mystics, and monastics were called from the established order and its maintenance in order to give themselves up entirely to God. Poverty, chastity, and obedience are all vows that renounce the end of maintaining the world. This is vividly expressed in chastity: no children no world, at least not the world occupied by the human family. The claim of the religious is that God is present outside of the maintenance of society and culture.

In the established world of Christianity, the religious bear witness to the call of God that life is not a matter of world maintenance. Instead, we know God in our poverty, in the abandoning of our dearest possessions, even that of children and family, good as they are in themselves. Instead, God is known in the embrace of all those in need because there we experience the primordial action of God as present now amid whatever suffering there is. God is present regardless of what happens if we but accept this presence in the embrace of the other. In other words, at the foundation of life is the covenant of hospitality.

The religious provide the clearest vision of the nature of God's calling. God's calling is the call to freedom. We don't have to worry finally about the end, about God abandoning us. We know God is calling us in the place and time now given to us. God is calling us in the common life in which we come to love and care. But God is also calling us in the darkness, at the edges, sometimes seemingly altogether apart from what we want to accomplish. We can, therefore, hear God's call only as we take time to dwell with God, in quiet and prayer, in hospitality to the stranger, in the work at hand, not as planning but as the way in which we care for one another.

The danger of identifying vocation with the religious is that their way of life becomes a "higher" way. As the religious cultivate the spiritual disciplines, the disciplines themselves are consecrated. Instead of means of hearing and deepening the call of God in daily life, they become ends in themselves.[4] Prayer, meditation, and contemplation are the pure knowledge of God. The end of life is then conceived as contemplation itself. This end is called the beatific vision, literally seeing and hence dwelling in beatitude, that which is the ultimate goodness of life. Examination of the self is intensified from self-abnegation (setting aside one's own interests in order to place oneself before God) to self-negation. Disciplines of examination become less matters of examination in order to hear anew the call of God than part of the disciplines of purgation. Examination seeks to purge worldly desire. As the word *purgation* suggests, instead of simplification of life in order to enable response, what stands at the center of the spiritual disciplines as a whole is a world-denying asceticism. The duties and actions that come to mark and deepen the religious life are then prayer, meditation, contemplation, confession, and purgation. Acts of hospitality remain obligations of the religious. However, again, these actions are no longer a response to God in the face of the stranger. They do not therefore deepen the sense and call of God in the world. What are traditionally

4. See Kenneth Kirk, *The Vision of God* (London: Longmans, Green and Co., 1932). Kirk interprets the Christian tradition in terms of the tension between a practical piety and a narrow focus on rules, a rigorist asceticism, and the institutions of the church.

called corporate acts of mercy or acts of charity are now more narrowly understood as preparing the soul for God.

As Martin Luther saw, the danger of the religious life was that the religious life substituted a self-cultivated piety for grace itself. A former Roman Catholic and Augustinian monk, Luther saw ascetics, mystics, and monastics escaping God's call in the world. Instead, all persons were priests in that all persons were Christ to others as they mediated the love of God to each other. Religious vocations were then rejected. The only true calling of God was work given in the world for the sake of the world. Work and daily life shared in community were thus endowed with a renewed dignity and worth. Work was hence approached with a seriousness we have come to associate with Protestantism.[5] In this way Luther, for example, speaks eloquently on the petition in the Lord's Prayer, "give us today our daily bread."[6] As with the earliest vision of vocation, work was not individual but was the way and place in which God was present to us, calling us beyond ourselves into community.

What became the danger within Protestantism, however, was that the way of the world became consecrated so that God's call was narrowed again to world maintenance. With the establishment of Protestantism as the religion of the state of the nations of northern Europe, the Protestant churches supported their supporters, just as the Roman Catholic Church had supported its own establishment ever since Constantine established Christianity in A.D. 312. The understanding of calling to work in the world was again understood as the work and roles given in society. These were simply viewed as divinely ordained, from the role of king as sovereign to the role of the lowest peasant as obedient servant.

A final narrowing of the sense of vocation happens with the narrowing of work in the modern economies. In these economies the pro-

5. See what remains as a classic, Max Weber's *The Protestant Ethic and the Spirit of Capitalism,* trans. Talcott Parsons (New York: Charles Scribner's, 1958), pp. 79-92.

6. Martin Luther, *The Large Catechism,* trans. Robert H. Fischer (Philadelphia: Fortress, 1959), pp. 74-76.

duction of goods and services is increasingly separated from a common life. The personal exchange of production, in barter or in buying and selling, is no longer experienced as service in a shared community. The work of the skilled craftsman as much as that of the factory worker or business person is narrowly a "job." A person labors in order to provide income that then might be used to provide the goods of life — clothing, food, and shelter, as well as entertainment and education. The professions themselves are understood more individualistically apart from service to the community. Law, medicine, and teaching might still be called vocations, but they are increasingly less a matter of calling to serve the community and more a matter of being called to what is individually fulfilling. Hence, all persons should have equal opportunity to pursue a profession.

The contemporary narrowing of vocation to work reflects a world fragmented into distinct and largely separate spheres: work and commerce, politics and the state, entertainment and sports, education and training, self-help and the therapeutic, friends and family, religion and culture. The longing for a greater connectedness, however, remains. This longing is evidenced by the hope that work might be something more than work, that it might be the means of service and even the transformation of the world into a world that is more just and loving. This concern is expressed in calls for renewing professions as civic occupations in which "the goal of self-actualization [is] . . . reoriented by integrating individual goals with those of the larger community."[7] However, such a focus on the renewal of vocation shows how much the idea of vocation is itself captive to the Protestant reduction of vocation to work, as if calling came from work itself. Vocation, however, was in its beginning never a matter of world maintenance.

From the perspective of Christian faith, an adequate understanding of work can happen only within the context of a life lived in response to God. In this sense, vocation as calling must be understood as a way of life lived in openness to God. The vocation of a Christian is in this sense nothing other than discipleship, fellowship in the way of

7. William Sullivan, *Work and Integrity* (San Francisco: Harper, 1995), p. 237.

Christ. The word vocation, though, may be the more apt word for the life of faith. The argument here is that we follow a distinctive way of life because we hear and respond to the call of the other to recognize and care for him or her. This call is Christian as it is revealed and effected in Christ. But always, the world of the other is the only world I have. I am not born with a world but am born into a world given in relationship to the other.

Whether near or distant, neighbor or stranger, the other calls me into life itself. The face of the other, given voice culturally, calls me to recognize and acknowledge him or her beyond my need and interest. The other calls me to recognize her in her otherness, in her uniqueness. This uniqueness can never be fully grasped. Her history is hers alone. It stretches behind me and can only be interpreted. It is never my own. Her aspirations in turn extend beyond what I know. They may inspire me precisely because they are not my own. Her perceptions and responses in the present can never then be simply predicted. She invites me into a new world. Call is the only way to comprehend this primordial experience of being. We are called into life. The Christian life is a way of life opened to the call of God.

The Faith of Piety

The traditional understanding of this practical piety has been that of duties towards oneself in daily life, towards the neighbor in love and justice, and towards God in prayer and worship. As a matter of hospitality, the personal language of relationships more adequately construes this life than the language of duties. There is no situation in which we are devoid of the presence of God — in poverty and prosperity, in sickness and in health, in our dying as well as in our living. We may have failed to respond to the presence and call of God. Our lives may have contracted until they were defined narrowly in terms of our self-preservation. Amidst the brokenness of our lives, however, the presence and call of God remains.

This new world into which I am called is not another world separate from the world I have known. Rather, the call of God is a call by which the world in which I live is transformed. My child is no longer an extension of myself, my hope and salvation, the means by which all that I love is born into the future. Instead, the child is a gift, a stranger who invites me to acknowledge her and draws me into wonder and delight at her world. Similarly, the sick and those in need are not a threat to my well-being but companions who are my well-being. What is important is different. Wealth and honor cease to define me. Priorities change. Life is simplified. I am not always in role, responding to the world in terms of my position in life, often meeting expectations in the constant effort to maintain my style of life. Instead, I am able to stop and listen to the voices around me, including my own. In the extreme, what appears as poverty to the world — a renunciation of wealth and position — is a holy simplicity open to the call of God.

I have heard this call in the face of others and known its demand in the laws that speak of justice. This call has been revealed to me, as a Christian, as the call of God into new life in the life, teaching, and ministry of Jesus as that culminates in his crucifixion, death, and resurrection. I have heard this call in scripture, especially in the context of prayer and worship. In worship I hear the Word of God and in prayer enact that Word in offering myself to God. This offering is most fully expressed in the Eucharist. There I am drawn into a new covenant, a covenant of hospitality. And what is revealed and known in worship is realized in the distinctive practices of hospitality, what I have called sacramental acts, none more central than table fellowship, the forgiveness of sins, and the care for the sick and those in need.

The Lord's Prayer gives voice to this faith. First is the acknowledgment of God. ("Our Father in Heaven, hallowed be your name.") We then entrust ourselves to God in all of life ("Your kingdom come, your will be done"), even in the midst of our limitations and frailty. ("Give us today our daily bread . . . save us from the time of trial and deliver us from evil.") At the heart of this faith is the embrace of God. We cannot then help but embrace one another. The Lord's Prayer centers on this fact. We pray that we may acknowledge and accept this embrace. This means entering into what I have called the covenant of hospitality. And so we pray, "Forgive us our sins as we forgive those who have sinned against us." Forgiven, we forgive; loved, we love.

Scripture offers a range of witnesses that illumine the character of
faith as an entrusting of ourselves to God. Abraham commended himself to God in giving up his personal hopes in his willingness to sacrifice
his son Isaac. Similarly, Joseph, "the dreamer," saw beyond the petty
concerns of his brothers. He opened himself to others and to possibilities
for the future. In Egypt Moses broke away from his security as a member
of the royal household, and led his people out of slavery to become a new
people marked by hospitality to the stranger. Amos and Jeremiah re-
sponded to the breaking of the bonds of this covenant by giving themselves over to the demands of justice. Ruth heard this call to love and
abide beyond any particular society, and thus she went with her mother-
in-law, Naomi, to the land of Israel. And, of course, the list goes on —
from the witnesses in scripture to the saints living and dead.

There is no single virtue that describes this life of hospitality. Instead, to respond to the call of God and to enter into the covenant of
hospitality results in a complex of attitudes and dispositions. Paul, for
example, speaks of the fruits of the Spirit: love, joy, peace, patience,
kindness, generosity, faithfulness, gentleness, and self-control (Gal.
5:22, 23). These are suggestive but by no means exhaustive or systematic in describing the character of our response to the call of God. As
the character of our response is formed in response to the particular
situations in which we find ourselves, the description itself varies.
Sometimes one and sometimes another virtue is heightened.[8]

8. See pp. 16-18 above for an initial account of virtue as habit, expressed
traditionally in terms of the theological virtues of faith, hope, and love and of the
cardinal virtues of temperance, fortitude/courage, prudence/practical wisdom,
and justice. In contrast to the account grounded in the Aristotelian and Neo-
Platonic understandings of Thomas Aquinas, the distinctiveness of this account
of the Christian life is evidenced in the virtues, which depict the response given
in the experience of God in the other — most notably in trust, vulnerability, and
hospitality. For a description of the eschatological virtues as primary to the Christian life, see Bernard Häring, *Free and Faithful in Christ. Vol. 1: General Moral
Theology* (New York: Seabury, 1978), pp. 201-8. More recently, grounded in a re-
lational view of the self, James F. Keenan proposed the virtues of justice, fidelity,
self-care, and prudence as the cardinal virtues. See Keenan, "Proposing Cardinal
Virtues," *Theological Studies* 56 (December 1995): 723-28.

The heart of the response to God is, though, a matter of entrusting ourselves to God in entering into the covenant of hospitality. Such is not itself something simply willed but is given in vulnerability and hospitality. Trust is given only as we know ourselves as strangers in a strange land, wandering Arameans, standing in poverty, ultimately naked, unable to secure our own existence, and yet welcomed and embraced. Only in our ultimate dependence on the other can we know and hence trust what gives life beyond us. Such dependence and trust is given in hospitality, as we are welcomed and as we welcome. In both cases we are in need of the other. In the welcoming embrace we are drawn out of ourselves into new life.

As Christians have gone on to claim, to entrust ourselves to God in hospitality is to experience love. Love is the experience of grace given in relationship with another. As such, love is a gift *(agape)* which fulfills our greatest longing *(eros),* and in fact passes all understanding. In faith, as a matter of trust, we are brought into a union *(philia),* a covenant, which alone is enduring. Nothing can separate us from the love of God. Faith and love are both gifts. They are not qualities that can be simply willed. This is most evident in the third enduring character of faith: hope. Christians neither despair nor resign themselves to whatever will be. Theirs is a hope that the world cannot know. They live into another world, the world of hospitality, which is already though not yet. As the Gospel of Mark concludes, Jesus the crucified is not at the tomb. He has been raised and is going ahead of us into Galilee (Mark 16:6, 7) and to the ends of the earth.

Ethics and the Christian Life

As piety is a matter of faith, the Christian life is not an ethic, if by an ethic is meant a moral handbook. Christian ethics is not about forming a single, universal ethic, a once-and-for-all account of all that we should do. Instead, as vocation, to speak of Christian ethics is to speak of a call that draws us into new relationships. The task of Christian ethics is to enable the call of God.

One task of ethics is to consider moral cases ranging from sexual relationships or medical treatment of the dying to the just use of force or the world economic order and third world debt. The purpose of casuistry, however, is not finding the right answer to a moral question, as if ethics were the application of theory to practice. Instead, the primary purpose of casuistry is practical, to illumine the particular moral conflicts we confront in order to make persons aware of what is at stake in the possible courses of action. In this sense, casuistry is not to resolve moral problems but to enable persons to listen and hear what is going on so that they may respond to the presence of God.[9] The consideration of cases can only serve this primary purpose when the broader understanding of Christian faith as a way of life is understood and kept in view. As distinct from casuistry, the task of Christian ethics — what is called moral theology — is to offer an account of the Christian life in order to deepen an understanding of how God is present in life.

Christian ethics as an account of the Christian moral life may be developed in different ways depending on how the presence of God is construed.[10] This itself is in part a matter of audience and what questions are most pressing. For example, the presence of God as given in the forgiveness of sins continues to speak to the experience of an order necessary for human life and of our personal failure to uphold and participate in this order. A Christian ethic may then be developed under the themes of God as judge and redeemer. The focus of such an ethic is likely to be justification by grace. In contrast, a different account of the moral life is needed to address those who are oppressed and marginalized by a political and economic order in which they are not recognized and where they are unable to participate in forming a

9. Recent scholarship has developed historical accounts of the history of casuistry that serve to illumine the nature of casuistry as a matter of practical moral reasoning. See Albert R. Jonsen and Stephen Toulmin, *The Abuse of Casuistry: A History of Moral Reasoning* (Berkeley: University of California Press, 1988); and John Mahoney, *The Making of Moral Theology: A Study of the Roman Catholic Tradition* (Oxford: Clarendon, 1987).

10. The classic study of Christian ethics in this manner is H. Richard Niebuhr's *Christ and Culture* (New York: Harper & Row, 1953). For a contemporary classic see James M. Gustafson, *Christ and the Moral Life* (New York: Harper & Row, 1968).

future world as a people. A Christian ethic of liberation may, therefore, be developed in terms of prophetic denunciation of the structures of oppression and a more pastoral annunciation of how life is to be lived freed from a cycle of dependence, violence, and counterviolence.[11] Still another account will be developed where the overwhelming concern is with the ecological crisis that threatens to destroy what the Book of Common Prayer calls "this fragile earth, our island home."[12] In this light the central themes of a Christian ethic might well be incarnation and the body of God.[13] The focus of the Christian life could then be developed in a variety of ways, for example, as a matter of coming to a sense of awe and reverence, blessing and thanksgiving, compassion and care.

Despite such differences, Christian ethics as an account of Christian faith and life will have at its center the transformation of life given in relationship to God. Regardless of the themes developed, this transformation will be a way of life incarnate in the world. This way of life will be marked by a sense of covenant in which individual wholeness and identity are given in participation in something larger than the self. And always, these accounts will be Christian to the extent that this new life is revealed and given in and through Jesus Christ. This is what I have meant by saying Christian faith is a life of practical piety that is incarnate, corporate, and sacramental.

As Christian, the life lived into God is grounded in the church. The church reveals as it draws persons into the story of Christ as the

11. The classic of liberation theology remains Gustavo Gutiérrez, *A Theology of Liberation,* trans. Sr. Caridad Inda and John Eagleson (Maryknoll, N.Y.: Orbis, 1973). For an introduction to contemporary North American liberation theologies, see review essays from different liberationist perspectives in Roger A. Badham, ed., *Introduction to Christian Theology* (Louisville, Ky.: Westminster/ John Knox, 1998), pp. 183-252.

12. *The Book of Common Prayer* (New York: Church Hymnal, 1982), p. 370.

13. See, for example, Sallie McFague, *The Body of God: An Ecological Theology* (Minneapolis: Fortress, 1993); Rosemary Radford Reuther, *Gaia and God: An Ecofeminist Theology of Earth Healing* (San Francisco: Harper, 1992); and James M. Gustafson, *A Sense of the Divine: The Natural Environment from a Theocentric Perspective* (Cleveland: Pilgrim, 1994).

story of our lives. This is always both a looking back and a drawing forward. As a looking back, the story of Christ is a recognition, a hearing of what sounds true, that our lives are plotted in suffering and freedom, failure and possibility, fear and hope, sorrow and joy, judgment and forgiveness, death and life. As a drawing forward, the story of Christ enacts the story in practices: in prayer and worship, through the examination and formation of our lives, and in those particular actions in which God's presence is given — specifically table fellowship, visiting and caring for the sick and those in need, and the forgiveness of sins. Together, as story and practices, as Word and sacrament, the church calls God's presence into our lives. In this sense, the calling of the church is the calling of God in our lives. Or to speak as a matter of faith, God calls persons to the church because the church is the way that draws them more deeply into the divine life.

In this introduction, the Christian moral life has been construed in terms of a covenant of hospitality. In the embrace of the other is the presence of God. Wholeness of life is given first of all in the family, to the extent that these first, most intimate relations of life are not means of securing a haven but invite us, rather, to embrace and care for the other as other. In turn, the covenant that gives wholeness to life is most poignantly revealed in voluntary poverty and hospitality. As Christians, we know and enter into this covenant anew through Jesus' life and teaching as that culminates in his dying and death. This happens through the story of scripture, in the proclamation and enactment of that story in worship, and by the practice of that faith in what are called disciplines or spiritual exercises. In this way we are raised with Christ, in Christ, and through Christ into eternal life. In this covenant we are a resurrected people who live out this covenant of hospitality in our daily lives.

Appendix

~

THE DESCRIPTION of the Christian life offered in the previous chapters rests on a critical assessment of the nature of Christian faith. Understanding Christian faith as a matter of practical piety is to see that the revelation given in the Christian story is nothing less than a new meaning and identity for our lives. This assumes that Christian faith is distinctive in content but is formed as is human identity in general in the interplay of narrative interpretations of life and the practices that constitute a life lived. This understanding of Christian faith as a practical piety grounded in the Christian story was first developed systematically by Friedrich Schleiermacher and then developed further in terms of the distinctive, transformative, revelatory character of Christian faith by Karl Barth. This understanding is also assumed and developed in contemporary Roman Catholic sacramental and liturgical theologies and in the post-Christendom theology and ethic of Stanley Hauerwas as informed by the Anabaptist tradition. In this appendix I want to offer a brief account of these judgments, thus placing this introduction to the Christian life in the larger context of contemporary theology and ethics.

Theology as Grounded in Piety

Two features central to what may be called "classical expressions of Christian faith" are problematic for contemporary accounts of Christian faith. First, classical Christian accounts assumed a teleological naturalism. Change was a matter of something moving towards its preestablished end. Whether the acorn or the sun and the wind, change was understood as a matter of something moving from potentiality to actuality, of fulfilling its purpose. Second, scripture was understood as the story of our lives in the context of the beginning and end of the world. In this sense, Christian faith is understood as tied to an account of the cosmos. Christian faith reveals the purposes or ends of human life in the context of the ends of the natural world. Only an account of the cosmos — from beginning to end, creation to conclusion — provides the ultimate context and hence end, expressing a unified purpose in all that happens. Adopted from Neo-Platonism, all things come from God, *ex nihilo,* and will return to God. In short, causality (understanding why things are the way they are) was understood teleologically and hence tied to cosmology (a description of all things teleologically).

Given such cosmological claims tied to Neo-Platonism, modern Christian thought can be viewed as an attempt to make sense of faith in terms of piety itself rather than in the context of cosmology. The "new" sciences, beginning in the sixteenth and seventeenth centuries, explained natural phenomena naturally without immediate reference to something's end. These explanations, in turn, challenged the cosmological beliefs that were assumed central to Christian faith.[1] For example, the celestial observations from Copernicus to Galileo made sense only by positing that the earth circles the sun and not vice versa.[2] This challenged understandings of a three-storied universe, created in

1. See Charles Taylor, *The Sources of the Self: The Making of the Modern Identity* (Cambridge, Mass.: Harvard University Press, 1989), esp. Part III, pp. 211-302.

2. For an account of this history of science, see James M. Lattis, *Between Copernicus and Galileo* (Chicago: University of Chicago Press, 1994).

six days, in which the earth stood between hell beneath and heaven above, a universe in which humans were the center and crown of creation. Similarly, theories of evolution and more recently, understandings of genetics and reproduction account for plant and animal diversity in relation to environmental factors. A geological history of the earth accounts for the stratification of earth as revealed in mountains and streams. And ultimately a new cosmology develops that can explain observations from distant galaxies and beyond. The universe is understood as having begun in a "big bang" some 13 billion years ago and expanding in all directions ever since.

Altogether, the truth of Christian faith is not tied to a particular cosmology. Instead, the truth of faith arises from the experience of conversion, of change to a new life, which is then understood in light of understandings of the world and the cosmos.[3] As James Gustafson has modified Ernst Troeltsch's classic description of this relationship, "The idea of God is admittedly not directly accessible in any other way than by religious *piety*. Yet, the substantial content of ideas of God *cannot be incongruous (rather than must be 'in harmony')* with the other forms of scientific knowledge and also must be in some way indicated by these."[4] As such, Christian faith is understood critically as something other than a cosmological explanation.

Friedrich Schleiermacher was among the first theologians to offer such a critical account of Christian faith. Scripture and primary accounts of Christian faith — for example, Augustine's *Confessions* or Jeremy Taylor's *Holy Living* and *Holy Dying* — arise from the experience of what is redemptive. Accounts of faith as accounts of the cosmos are derivative. They are in this sense mythic. They give expression to the experience of redemption by articulating the human experience

---

3. See Stephen Toulmin, *The Return to Cosmology: Postmodern Science and the Theology of Nature* (Berkeley: University of California Press, 1982).

4. Ernst Troeltsch, "Religion and the Science of Religion," *Ernst Troeltsch: Writings on Theology and Religion,* Robert Morgan and Michael Pye, eds. (Atlanta: John Knox, 1977), p. 117; and James M. Gustafson, *Ethics from a Theocentric Perspective. Vol. 1: Theology and Ethics* (Chicago: University of Chicago Press, 1981), compare p. 251 and p. 257 as noted by the italics.

of redemption as a cosmic drama and, in turn, by attributing to God attributes necessary as the divine agent in the drama. As Edward Farley writes:

> Nineteenth-century liberal Protestant theology did not shun the theological task of articulating divine symbolics but it did change the basis of the derivation. At this point Schleiermacher is a seminal figure. He turns the enterprise from speculation and natural theology back to "religious" concerns, and (like the classical tradition itself) denies that attributes express knowledge *(Erkenntnis)* of God's nature *(Wesen)*. Also like the classical view, he retains the method of causality but alters it from God as world-causality to God as that which transforms the formal anthropological structure of utter dependence into redemptive God-consciousness. This anthropological structure of formal piety reappears in the mode of the sensible self-consciousness in an actual religious community. Thus the experience of redemption through Christ opens up the way to attributive language. We have here a deriving of attributes from the divine causality of redemption.[5]

More broadly, as variously developed in contemporary theology, Schleiermacher sought to ground faith in the experience of God, what has been designated the sacred, and to determine how this personal experience provides a ground or grounding that sanctifies life. As an interpretation of the tension between law and grace, for example, Schleiermacher argued that the experience of the sacred was the experience of absolute dependence which led the human person from a narrow self-determination to the love of the other.[6] A danger in such

---

5. Edward Farley, *Divine Empathy: A Theology of God* (Minneapolis: Fortress, 1996), p. 86. See Friedrich Schleiermacher, *The Christian Faith,* trans. H. R. Mackintosh and J. S. Steward (Edinburgh: T. & T. Clark, 1928), #50-52, pp. 194-206; also see Robert Williams, *Schleiermacher the Theologian: The Construction of the Doctrine of God* (Philadelphia: Fortress, 1978).

6. See Schleiermacher, *The Christian Faith,* #4-5, pp. 12-25. Following Schleiermacher in an argument from piety, and specifically the experience of ab-

theologies is a narrow focus on the experience of faith itself apart from how it is mediated or revealed and how it then reconciles and changes the individual in relationship to the world. Such a narrow focus on the experience of faith leads to what Ernst Troeltsch calls modern forms of mysticism.[7] As in the case of liberal theologies, equally inadequate are theologies that have turned back to uncritical accounts of Christian faith as cosmology by identifying the experience of faith with a moral ideal that is then projected as the end of history.[8]

Following Schleiermacher more than he acknowledged, Karl Barth shares the understanding that Christian faith has its ground in piety. As Kierkegaard stood Hegel on his head in beginning with the radical subjectivity of faith instead of the universalism of reason, Barth began within the circle of faith with revelation in order that the experience of faith was not abstracted and universalized as a matter of human experience in general. As argued by Nigel Biggar, for Barth Christian faith is first and always a matter of "love and practice," an "affective and pragmatic reorientation or conversion" rather than a matter of knowledge about the nature of things.[9] In this sense Barth is not detailing Christian belief but is describing faith as a way of life begun, sustained, and renewed in Jesus Christ. Barth's evangelical theology is, in this sense, like Schleiermacher's, not a philosophy of faith

---

solute dependence, see H. Richard Niebuhr, *The Responsible Self* (New York: Harper & Row, 1963), esp. pp. 108-26.

7. Ernst Troeltsch, *The Social Teachings of the Christian. Vol. II,* trans. Olive Wyon (Louisville, Ky.: Westminster/John Knox, 1992), pp. 791-99.

8. Walter Rauschenbusch exemplified such liberal theologies. See his *A Theology for the Social Gospel* (Louisville, Ky.: Westminster/John Knox, 1997), pp. 95-109, 131-45. Chapter 10 grounds Christian faith in piety while in chapter 13 faith is grounded in the kingdom of God as an ethical ideal. Reinhold Niebuhr criticizes liberalism's moral idealism but still expresses his understanding of Christian faith in terms of moral ideals. See *An Interpretation of Christian Ethics* (Harper & Brothers, 1935), p. 15 and then p. 37; see also Reinhold Niebuhr, *The Nature and Destiny of Man. Vol. II: Human Destiny* (New York: Charles Scribner's Sons, 1943), pp. 68-76.

9. Nigel Biggar, *The Hastening that Waits: Karl Barth's Ethics* (Oxford: Clarendon, 1993), p. 11.

but a thick, concrete description of Christian faith as a way of life. Unlike Schleiermacher, the constructive promise of this evangelical theology is that it returns the listener or reader to the story and life in which faith is given.

What is crucial in Barth's evangelical theology is the shape of the Christian story. For Barth, reflecting the Reformed tradition, what is normative is not *imitatio Christi,* the imitation of Christ, with primary emphasis on cross and self-sacrifice. Such a view of Christian faith had privileged the passion, the suffering Christ, apart from the larger proclamation of creation and redemption. "Self-sacrifice is not the principle of Christian life."[10] Instead, for Barth what is central to the Christian narrative as gospel, as good news and saving knowledge, is humanity before God as Creator, Reconciler, and Redeemer, a theme he develops in terms of humanity before God in fellowship, for life, and in limitation.[11] The basis of this account is both evangelical and catholic: it is transformative and it corresponds to tradition, to the apostolicity and catholicity of the church.

Roman Catholic sacramental theology has provided an account of faith analogous to that of contemporary Protestant thought from Schleiermacher to Barth.[12] Again, both understand Christian faith as practical piety, as a way of life that is given from within the circle of faith, where the warrants for faith are its transformative power and its correspondence to tradition. Karl Rahner offers the most systematic understanding of this piety.[13] Like Schleiermacher, he turns to the subject in order to articulate the experience of faith. This he describes as the experience of incomprehensible mystery, in light of which hu-

10. Biggar, pp. 108, 109.

11. See Karl Barth, *Church Dogmatics. III/4: The Doctrine of Creation* (Edinburgh: T. & T. Clark, 1961), table of contents, p. xv.

12. As central to the development of contemporary Roman Catholic sacramental theology, see Edward Schillebeeckx, *Christ: The Sacrament of the Encounter with God,* trans. Paul Barrett (New York: Sheed and Ward, 1963). On the nature of sacramental theology as grounded in piety, see Aidan Kavanagh, *On Liturgical Theology* (New York: Pueblo, 1984), pp. 73-121.

13. Karl Rahner, *Foundations of Christian Faith,* trans. William V. Dych (New York: Seabury, 1978), pp. 75-89, 126-37.

mans experience their lives in terms of freedom and dependence, self-determination and suffering. True freedom comes in the acknowledgment of this mystery and then in trust entering into this mystery. For Christians this happens through Jesus, specifically as Jesus' response of self-offering is enacted by us in worship in general and the Eucharist in particular.[14]

Formed in faith as a Jesuit through the Ignatian spiritual exercises, Rahner viewed the passion narratives as central to Christian faith;[15] however, with Barth they are not opposed to the larger biblical narratives. Instead, they reveal the nature of creation itself. What distinguishes Rahner's theology from Barth is that the biblical narrative is understood first of all through the lens of worship, specifically Eucharist as the central form of worship in the church. These narratives of worship are primary because they effect the transformation and reconciliation that stand at the heart of Christian faith. Despite their differences, Barth and Roman Catholic sacramental theology share in common the understanding that Christian faith is a matter of conversion and reconciliation grounded in a narrative identity given in Christ as concluded in cross and resurrection. Both understand that Christian faith is given as a matter of piety arising from the Christian

14. See Karl Rahner, "The Eucharist and Suffering," *Theological Investigations. Vol. 3*, trans. Karl-H. and Boniface Kruger (Longdon: Darton, Longman & Todd, 1967), pp. 161-70; and "The Eucharist and Our Daily Lives," *Theological Investigations. Vol. 7*, trans. David Bourke (London: Darton, Longman & Todd, 1971), pp. 211-26. On Rahner and Schillebeeckx and their turn to the subject and consequent understanding of worship in terms of symbolic causality in which the human person responds to the symbolic presentation of the faith, see David N. Power, *Unsearchable Riches: The Symbolic Nature of Liturgy* (New York: Pueblo, 1984), pp. 196-205. On suffering and sacrifice as the human response of faith, see Gordon W. Lathrop, *Holy Things: A Liturgical Theology* (Minneapolis: Fortress, 1993), pp. 139-58. For my own earlier development of such an understanding, see Timothy F. Sedgwick, *Sacramental Ethics: Paschal Identity and the Christian Life* (Philadelphia: Fortress, 1987), pp. 38-52.

15. See Karl Rahner, *Spiritual Exercises* (London: Sheed & Ward, 1965) and "On the Spirituality of the Easter Faith," *Theological Investigations. Vol. 17*, trans. Margaret Kohl (London: Darton, Longman & Todd, 1981), pp. 8-15.

story grounded in scripture and effected in the reading of scripture and in worship.

The central place of the Christian story in effecting Christian faith as piety, as a way of life, has been further argued by Stanley Hauerwas. Drawing on the Anabaptist tradition, Hauerwas sees Christian faith given as narrative identity, as the Christian story is lived in daily life.[16] What stands at the center of this story for Hauerwas is the renunciation of power as the instrument of history, as the means of achieving identity through achieving some particular state of affairs. Instead, life is given in the renunciation of power and the welcoming embrace of those who form our life — family, friends, and strangers. The "saving story" of scripture is known in the living of that story, specifically in the imitation of Christ as exemplified in nonviolence and hospitality.[17]

Again, the contemporary theological accounts of Christian belief representing Protestant, Roman Catholic, and Anabaptist traditions are contemporary in rejecting the truth of Christian faith as truths of cosmology and instead understanding them as the truth of a life-giving practical piety. Central to these accounts is the narrative character of Christian faith, that is to say, the relationship of the story of Christian faith as given in scripture and worship (Word and sacrament) and the practice of faith as lived.

Narrative Theology and Practice

Among contemporary theorists, Paul Ricoeur has given one of the more comprehensive analyses of narrative and its relationship to human action.[18] As described in Aristotle's *Poetics,* narrative is a matter of the de-

16. Stanley Hauerwas, *A Community of Character* (Notre Dame: University of Notre Dame Press, 1981), esp. pp. 36-52, 89-128; and *The Peaceable Kingdom: A Primer in Christian Ethics* (Notre Dame: University of Notre Dame Press, 1983), pp. 24-34.

17. Hauerwas, *The Peaceable Kingdom,* pp. 72-95.

18. Paul Ricoeur, *Oneself as Another,* trans. Kathleen Blamey (Chicago: University of Chicago Press, 1992), pp. 113-68.

velopment of character in terms of a plot.[19] A set of conflicts generates a plot in which character is both revealed and developed. For example, in classical tragedy a conflict reveals the character and tragic flaw of the protagonist. Agamemnon's sense of obligation to his city and to the men who have gathered to go to war in order to free Helen comes into conflict with his duties as a father. He tragically must sacrifice his daughter Iphigenia to appease the goddess Artemis if the fleet is to set sail for Troy. Character is revealed and developed in the "emplotment."

In the scriptural narratives, character may be understood as revealed and developed in the conflict between idolatry as a matter of particular human concerns and loyalties and faithfulness to God as its opposite, in the sense of the experience of an identity beyond those particular loyalties. For example, for Abraham faithfulness to God comes into conflict with his love of his son Isaac when he hears God calling him to sacrifice Isaac (Gen. 22:1-14). The character of Abraham's faithfulness, and so faithfulness itself, is revealed and developed in this drama, especially as the story is retold and developed by Søren Kierkegaard.[20] Understood as the drama between faithfulness and idolatry, the stories of the prophets are further developments of this plot and so reveal other perspectives on faithfulness. The book of Job, in turn, explores and develops the understanding of idolatry and faithfulness in still another way. For Christians, Jesus is then the culminating story of faithfulness.

The events that generate a plot are the conflicts of life itself. The events are narrated as the story of how persons are acted upon and how they act. In these acts a person's identity is revealed, challenged, and formed, lost, changed, or sustained.[21] As Ricoeur says, narratives answer the question of "permanence in time."[22]

The adequacy of a narrative identity is a matter of its capacity to

---

19. Ricoeur, p. 143. Ricoeur's term is "emplotment."

20. Søren Kierkegaard, *Fear and Trembling* and *The Sickness Unto Death*, trans. Walter Lowrie (Princeton, N.J.: Princeton University Press, 1941), pp. 22-132.

21. Ricoeur, p. 147; see pp. 141-47.

22. Ricoeur, p. 116.

illumine and make sense of the experience and understandings of persons. This means that in addition to a person's autobiographical experience, narrative identity must make sense, or at least not contradict, the range of narratives and other beliefs that form the understandings of a person. Central to such comprehension, narrative identity must comprehend the range of narratives and other documents that form scripture, the witnesses of the tradition, and understandings of the world (from causality to cosmology, from psychology to society).[23] For example, as developed by Thomas Aquinas, the unifying metaphor of the vision of God makes just this kind of sense of the medieval world. Luther's justification by faith makes sense of the radicalness of grace in a world that was broken apart by the radical sense of sin and the loss of confidence in a unifying order to things. In liberal theologies, the kingdom of God draws together a unified understanding in which otherworldly conceptions of faith are denied and where the optimism of a progressive development is assumed.

This description of narrative in terms of character and plot enables Ricoeur to illumine the relationship between a story told and a life lived. As the narration of events, a story is always retrospective, a telling of events that have happened.

Our lives, however, are never a matter of the imitation of a story. The conflicts we confront are never exact duplicates of those narrated from the past. We therefore project our identity into the future in terms of an imagined constancy of action. We see ourselves as acting in certain ways that express the character we see revealed in the stories that we accept as the story of our lives. But how we actually respond is always something different than what is projected.[24]

The constancy of actions that we imagine as expressions of our character may be called practices.[25] A shipbuilder is one who builds

23. See note 4 above.

24. Ricoeur, pp. 157-63, which includes criticism of Alasdair MacIntyre who assumes "a narrative unity to life" in *After Virtue: A Study in Moral Theory,* (Notre Dame: University of Notre Dame Press, 1984), pp. 204-25.

25. On the nature of practices and their prenarrative quality, see Ricoeur, pp. 152-57.

ships. A citizen is one who participates in the affairs of the state. A parent is one who raises children. A good shipbuilder, citizen, or parent is the person who does these actions well. The actions that make a shipbuilder, a citizen, or a parent are neither self-determined nor singular. No two ships are alike. New challenges confront each citizen. Children are never the same. Moreover, to be a shipbuilder, citizen, or parent is not to do one thing but a variety of acts that are connected by some larger sense of purpose. For example, in the case of a cook, cooking is not some one thing but a variety of acts that are related together in terms of some broader meanings. Cooking includes establishing a menu, procuring foods, preparation of ingredients, baking, broiling, or boiling, and finally presentation and serving. Each act opens up as well as limits other acts in light of an envisioned outcome. My menu determines what foods I will purchase, but the available foods determine the menu. Similarly, the menu and time required for preparation determine the order of service and presentation, although preparation and the sense of presentation affect the choice of food for the menu in the first place. And what is true of cooking is equally true of shipbuilding, citizenship, and parenting.

As character is both revealed and developed in the human response to events, the unfinished or open-ended relationship between acts in forming and sustaining a practice indicates that character is not fixed or final. This is all the more true as the practices that form my life as a whole are many. The unity of the self as a unity of purposes depends then on some ongoing development of these practices into what has been called a life plan or a way of life that would give unity to the larger unfinished "story" of our lives. In old age, for example, the character I have formed as a parent and in my profession is now in crisis. My children have grown up and are living on their own. I have retired. Having given up my professional work, I begin to garden or cook or serve in new ways in the community. I read and write. I cultivate friendships. I mentor and grandparent. The actions I undertake no longer cluster together in the same way as previously. They cluster together in new ways, and I begin to understand the practices of my life differently. What it means to love and serve now seems different. As I understand the practices of my life differently I understand the stories that have interpreted my life differently, perhaps as still true but now with more nuance or "more fully." There is here a dialectic between narratives and practices; each informs the other.

At the level of meanings and purposes, the Christian story describes the conflicts of loyalties and realities and resolves this conflict in terms of some larger meaning and purpose. In this way the Christian story calls for me to conform my life to this vision. Certain practices — such as worship, hospitality, forgiveness, and table fellowship — draw together acts in terms of a sense of this vision. In this sense Christian faith is not an idea or a belief but always a practice, a way of life — what I have called a practical piety. Further, the life lived remains open-ended, unfinished, in process, such that Christian faith is not identical with a singular interpretation of the Christian story and a corresponding set of practices. Rather, Christian faith is the life lived in which the revelation of the story is experienced in part but can never be experienced fully. This is what is meant by speaking of Christian faith as always eschatological, already but not yet, something lived into but not completed.

Understandings of God

Returning to the question of narrative identity, the dialectic internal to narratives and between narrative understandings and practices is drawn together in terms of unifying metaphors or what may be called root metaphors.[26] These metaphors construe the enduring relationship with God and often signify the ending of the narrative, the resolving of the conflicts that constitute the story. To the extent that the story is a model for the reader, these metaphors indicate how human persons should relate to life's events. Some of the central unifying metaphors in the Christian tradition have been the vision of God, the king-

26. On the nature of metaphors in theology, see Sallie McFague, *Metaphorical Theology: Models of God and Religious Language* (Philadelphia: Fortress, 1983). More broadly, see David Tracy, *The Analogical Imagination: Christian Theology and the Culture of Pluralism* (New York: Crossroad, 1981), pp. 405-45.

dom of God, justification by grace, eternal life, *theosis,* covenant, love, freedom, and liberation.[27]

Different narrative identities are further distinguished by different conceptions of God. That is to say, divine attributes are the metaphors by which God is understood given the narrative understanding of identity. For example, the Christian narrative is interpreted by Thomas Aquinas in light of a Neo-Platonic cosmology and an Aristotelian metaphysic. As Being, God is the first and final cause, the beginning and end of what is. Given such understandings, the scriptural narrative is read in terms of creation, fall, and redemption. Creation as history is a matter of exit and return *(exitus et reditus).* All comes from and will return to God. Given this narrative cosmology, God is the perfection of what is (pure act or actuality). From this it is a logical step to say that God is all-powerful, all-knowing, and present everywhere — omnipotent, omniscient, and omnipresent. More personally, God acts upon us and calls us into relation. The end of our lives, imaged as the vision of God, is response to this God, and ultimately it is to know, love, and rest in God.

In contrast to understandings in which the vision of God is the unifying metaphor, in Protestant thought the scriptural narrative is understood in terms of the unifying metaphor of justification by faith. God is not Being but is first and last experienced as the power or will that shapes our lives, as judgment and as grace. We know God in the movement of our lives from sin into salvation. God is the sovereign ruler who judges and redeems, who as good is a God of mercy and love. Despite the differences, in both Thomistic and Protestant understandings, God is personal and loving, ruler, judge, and redeemer. Both assume a Neo-Platonic cosmology where all things come from

27. Classic accounts that offer such construals of Christian faith in terms of different basic or root metaphors include Anthony Flew, *The Idea of Perfection in Christian Theology: An Historical Study* (London: Oxford, 1934); James M. Gustafson, *Christ and the Moral Life* (New York: Harper & Row, 1968); Kenneth Kirk, *The Vision of God* (London: Longmans, Green and Co., 1931); and Frederick Denison Maurice, *The Kingdom of Christ,* 2 vols., ed. Alex R. Vidler (London: SCM, 1958), esp. vol. 1, pp. 41-138.

and return to God. For both, humans stand at the center of a cosmological drama where God is sovereign, a personal will which is omnipotent, omniscient, and omnipresent.

What so distinguishes narrative identities after the eighteenth century is the questioning of the Neo-Platonic cosmology in light of the new sciences and understandings of the world. On the one hand, "fundamentalists" assume that Christian truths are historical, scientific truths about the cosmos. Christian narrative is not given as a matter of practical piety, which is then interpreted cosmologically. Instead, Christian narrative is first of all a supernatural revelation of cosmology, the meaning of which is "literal." On the other hand, liberals understand Christian truths as matters of practical piety that are understood in light of contemporary views of human history and the cosmos. In the modern liberal understandings of Christian faith, covenant is the unifying metaphor. God calls the human person and community into covenant. Christian faith and life are given in this covenant of love. God is understood specifically in terms of love itself. As the contemporary hymn says, "God himself is love, and where true love is God himself is there."[28] This focuses the understanding of God in terms of human fulfillment. Covenant with God is understood as the promise that love will prevail. This optimism correlates with an optimistic, progressive sense of history. The metaphor of covenant is thereby tied to a new evolutionary cosmology expressed by the metaphor of the kingdom of God.

The horrors of the twentieth century have made optimistic, liberal thought untenable. After Auschwitz and the other genocides of the twentieth century, Christian faith cannot be tied to the fulfillment of some ideal state of affairs in history. Given innocent suffering, history cannot be redeemed through appeal to some end. The horrors remain horrors, moral evils that call out for acknowledgment. To turn to some end and claim that history is thereby redeemed is to deny the radical evil of these horrors. For these postmoderns, the promise of fulfillment is no longer tied to an outcome in or beyond history. The image of the kingdom of God, therefore, drops from view. More resonant

28. *The Hymnal* (New York: Church Hymnal, 1982), p. 577.

with Job than with the Deuteronomic historian and the prophets, the metaphor of covenant shifts from love as a relationship to be realized to love as the recognition and respect for the other as other. The future is opened as grace but the outcome is beyond human understanding. God is less the power in which history is brought to fulfillment and more the power and structure of history expressed in the creativity and novelty that continue to unfold in the vast, complex relations that are creation.

Such contemporary understandings of Christian faith are more theocentric than anthropocentric, less to do with human well-being and more to do with a sense of wonder in the process of life that transcends human life. God is still understood as personal, as acting upon humans, but not as a sovereign power with a particular will or agency distinct or separate from creation itself, or as the power within history to bring about fulfillment. Instead of viewing God as King, Lord, or Ruler, God is understood as inviting and calling humanity to participate — as co-creator, as friend, and as fellow sufferer in the process of creation.[29]

Contemporary understandings of faith do not have a single, unifying narrative identity. In turn, there is no unifying metaphor for God, and no simple coherence between narrative accounts of the world and understandings of the cosmos. New metaphors for understanding God often gain their power in juxtaposition to previous metaphors. For example, God is friend rather than sovereign power. God as sovereign power is inadequate to modern understandings of the cosmos and to the human experience of the divine. Friendship construes God more deeply related to human life. However, friendship fails to comprehend the otherness of God. The metaphor of sovereignty thus continues to convey a truth about the experience and nature of God. God is not the object of human fulfillment but a power in its own right, under its own rule, to which humans are subject.[30]

29. For a systematic development of such understandings and a review of literature, see Farley, *Divine Empathy*.

30. Contrast, for example, Sallie McFague, *Models of God* (Philadelphia: Fortress, 1987), in which she argues for friendship as a model for understanding God with James M. Gustafson, *Ethics from a Theocentric Perspective, Vol. 1* (Chi-

The development of the symbolics of God is one of the tasks of philosophical and systematic theologies. Such a development of the doctrine of God is not, however, the task of this book. Rather, the focus of this book is on the experience of God as given and deepened in the Christian community of faith. As a way of life, this account is a matter of practical piety. The unifying or root metaphor in this account is covenant of hospitality.[31] As a matter of covenant, this metaphor focuses on the experience of God given in the relationships that form human life. As a matter of hospitality, this metaphor places difference at the heart of this relationship. Identity is given in difference. The relationships that form and give life are marked by "otherness." To be in relationship is then to enter into a continuing process of change or conversion, to be drawn outside of oneself, into what Karl Rahner speaks of as the incomprehensible mystery of being.

The argument of this book is that the metaphor of covenant of hospitality makes sense of what Christians speak of as the integral relationships between love of God and neighbor. More fully, the metaphor of covenant of hospitality is developed and tested in terms of understanding the relationships that form our life, specifically sexual relationships and our relationships with strangers. The character and practices central to this life include an account of the nature of worship, the problem of idolatry, the character of law and the meaning of gospel, the place of forgiveness, and the central place of "calling" in understanding the Christian life. More than an argument for the metaphor of covenant of hospitality, however, the purpose of this book is to offer an account of the Christian life that may serve in the deepening of practical piety.

---

cago: University of Chicago Press, 1981), in which the sovereignty of God is emphasized.

31. For an initial development of hospitality as central to understanding Christian faith, see Thomas W. Ogletree, *Hospitality to the Stranger* (Philadelphia: Fortress, 1985), esp. pp. 35-63. For a fuller development, see Edward Farley, *Good and Evil: Interpreting a Human Condition* (Minneapolis: Fortress, 1990), esp. pp. 31-46. Central to such works is the work of Emmanuel Levinas, *Totality and Infinity: An Essay on Exteriority,* trans. Alphonso Lingis (Pittsburgh: Duquesne University Press, 1969), esp. pp. 187-247.

Index

Anglican: Benedictine communities, 29-31; Book of Common Prayer, 31-32, 34, 37; ethics, 46-51; as practical piety, 27-29, 33-34, 51, 53; reformation, 33-34; theology, 34-43; worship, 30-33, 37-38, 46-51

Anglican thinkers: Joseph Butler, 38-39, 47, 50; Thomas Cranmer, 31, 34; John Donne, 39, 46; T. S. Eliot, 39; George Herbert, 32, 39, 41, 46; Richard Hooker, 35-39, 46, 48-49; David Hume, 47; John Keble, 48; Kenneth Kirk, 42, 49; William Law, 47; C. S. Lewis, 39; John Locke, 47; F. D. Maurice, 38-39, 50; John Henry Newman, 48; Edward Pusey, 48; Jeremy Taylor, 3, 39-41, 46-47, 49, 145; William Temple, 28, 38-39, 44, 49; R. S. Thomas, 39; Desmond Tutu, 42-43, 99; John Wesley, 41-42, 47-48; William Wilberforce, 41

Anthony, 85

Aristotle, 16, 150

Aquinas, Thomas, 28, 45, 152, 155

Augustine, 14, 108, 145

Barth, Karl, 143, 147-49

Basil the Great, 85, 87-89

Biggar, Nigel, 147

Bonhoeffer, Dietrich, 122

Brown, Peter, 82

Calvin, John, 18, 64

Christian Ethics: as an account of the Christian life, 49-50, 139-41; Anglican, 46-51; as casuistry, 15, 46-47, 138-39; as enabling response, 40, 138; Protestant, 18-21; questions of, 8; Roman Catholic, 14-18, 21

Confession, 14-15, 108-9

Conscience, 97-98

Covenant of hospitality, 141, 158; as ground of justice, 94, 95, 97, 99-101; in marriage and celibacy, 58-63, 70-76; and the poor, 80-89; as welcoming the stranger, 77-80, 131; worship and practices, 120-25, 136; and virtue, 137-38

INDEX

Eucharist: Anglican understandings of, 31-32, 37-38, 49; as idolatry, 121; meanings of, 116-20; as practice, 114-16; as sacrifice, 117-21

Farley, Edward, 146
Forgiveness, 14-15, 123-25
Freud, Sigmund, 64

Gandhi, Mahatma, 99
Geertz, Clifford, 98
Gustafson, James, 145

Hauerwas, Stanley, 143, 150
Hegel, Georg Wilhelm, 147
Human rights, 91

Idolatry: nature of, 62-69; as misplaced love, 21, 60; in worship, 121-22

Jesus: as Christ, 9; and covenant of hospitality, 82-84, 94, 120; and gospel, 100; and poverty, 83, 85; as revelation, 21, 29, 50-51, 58, 69-70, 147; as sacrament, 29, 38, 49, 51, 115-17; 120; as sacrifice, 83-84, 120; and sexuality, 58, 60-61

Justice: basic justice, 90-91; definition, 90; distributive, 91-93; foundations of, 94-96; and law, 95-100; love and, 94-95, 99-100; procedural, 93-94; questions of, 80-90; universality of, 98-99; as virtue, 16

Kierkegaard, Søren, 59, 147, 151
King, Martin Luther, 99

Law: and gospel, 18-20, 100-101; and justice, 95-100; natural and divine, 99; summary of (the Great Commandment), 10, 38, 94-95; Torah, 10-12, 100

Levinas, Emmanuel, 95
Lord's Prayer, 10, 120, 136
Love: as gift, 19-20, 138; the Great Commandment (as summary of the law), 10, 38, 94-95; as hospitality, 62, 80, 88-89, 138; and justice, 94-95, 99-100; and marriage, 71-72; and poverty, 88-89; and sexuality, 54-63; types of, 58-59, 62-63, 72, 138; as virtue, 17
Luther, Martin, 18, 20, 133, 152

Marriage, 58-60, 61-62, 70-74

Narrative identity: metaphors, 154-58; narrative, 150-52; in relation to human action, 152-54
Norms and principles, 66-68

Pachomius, 86, 89
Piety: Anglican account of, 29-43; Christian faith as, 27-29, 135-38, 140-41; 143, 149-50, 154, 158; definition, 3; as incarnational, corporate, sacramental, 27-29, 34, 39, 51, 140; types, 4-9
Plato, 16, 104
Pope John XXIII, 22
Poverty: in ancient Israel, 82; in the early church, 85-88; Jesus, 83-85; in late antiquity, 80-82
Practices: and ascesis, 110; confession, 108-9; denial and simplification, 109-11, 123; examination, 106-9, 123; meditation and contemplation, 105-6, 123; sacramental acts/duties, 110-14, 123, 136; as therapy, 104, 113-14; worship, 105-6, 114-16, 121
Prayer, 105-6, 123

Rahner, Karl, 148-49, 158

Ricoeur, Paul, 150-54

Sabbath, 11-14, 20, 129
Sacrament: Anglican understandings
    of, 37-38; Christ as, 29, 51, 101;
    church as, 101; definition, 28; as
    practice, 110-13; Word and, 21, 28,
    45, 50, 125, 145, 150
Sacrifice, 59-60, 62, 83-84, 117-21
Schleiermacher, Friedrich, 143, 145-
    48
Schillebeeckx, Edward, 101
Scripture: and Book of Common
    Prayer, 31; creation accounts, 55-
    56; and Eucharist, 49, 115; Gospel/
    grace, 48-49, 100; the Good Sa-
    maritan, 107-8; the Great Com-
    mandment, 10, 94-95; hospitality
    and the poor, 77-78, 82, 88, 119;
    Job, 78-79; Jesus and poverty, 80,
    85; Jesus and singleness of heart,
    83, 100; Jesus on sexuality; 58, 60-
    61; justice, 95; Lord's Prayer, 10,
    120, 136; and moral judgments,
    36-37; prophets and covenant, 79-
    80; render unto Ceasar, 130; sacri-
    fice, 117, 120; sacrifice of Isaac, 59-
    60; summary of the law, 10, 94-95;
    Ten Commandments, 11-12; To-
    rah, 10-11, 100
Sexuality: celibacy, 61; ends of, 57,
60-61, 73; desire and, 64; Genesis ac-
    counts, 55-56; Jesus, 58, 60-61; love
    and, 54, 56-63; norms and principles,
    66-68

Ten Commandments, 6, 9-14, 18, 20,
    63, 94, 125, 129
Theology: Anabaptist, 143, 150; Angli-
    can, 34-43, 46; and cosmology, 144-
    45, 156; ecumenical, 22-23; as
    grounded in redemption, 146-48; Ro-
    man Catholic sacramental, 143, 148-
    50; Roman Catholic and Protestant,
    21-22, types, 44-45
Troeltsch, Ernst, 145, 147

Virtues: cardinal, 16; fruits of the Holy
    Spirit, 19, 137; theological, 17, 138
Vocation: definition, 128; history of,
    130-34; and hearing God, 132-33; as
    response to God, 134-36, 138; and
    work, 128-29

Worship, 26, 103, 125-26; Anglican un-
    derstandings of, 29-38, 43; and the
    call of God, 131-32, 135-36, 141; and
    Eucharist, 49, 114-21; as idolatry,
    122; and narrative identity, 149-50;
    and the Sabbath, 12-14, 20; as sacra-
    mental practice, 105-6, 114-16, 121,
    158; as sacrifice, 117-21